EDUCATING THE PHYSICALLY HANDICAPPED

EDUCATING THE PHYSICALLY HANDICAPPED

An Investigation

T.M. Geetha

ANMOL PUBLICATIONS PVT. LTD.

NEW DELHI - 110 002 (INDIA)

ANMOL PUBLICATIONS PVT. LTD.
4374/4B, Ansari Road, Daryaganj
New Delhi - 110 002
Ph.: 23261597, 23278000
Visit us at: www.anmolpublications.com

Educating the Physically Handicapped

First Published, 2005

ISBN 81-261-2265-X

PRINTED IN INDIA

Published by J.L. Kumar for Anmol Publications Pvt. Ltd., New Delhi - 110 002 and Printed at Mehra Offset Press, Delhi.

CONTENTS

Preface *vii*

List of Tables *ix*

1. Introduction **1**

1.0 Introduction

1.1 Historical Background of Physically Handicapped Children

1.2 Concept of Physically Handicapped Children.

1.3 Concepts, Characteristics and Identification of Crippled Children

1.4 Adjustment Problems of the Crippled Children

1.5 Education of Exceptional Children

1.6 Education of the Crippled Children

1.7 Genesis of the Problem.

1.8 Statement of the Problem

1.9 Need and Importance of the Study.

1.10 Objectives of the Study.

1.11 An over View of the Study.

2. Review Of Related Literature **37**

2.1 Importance of Review of Related Literature.

2.2 Correlates of Achievement

2.2.1 Reviews Related to Self- Concept and Achievement.

2.2.2 Reviews Related to Anxiety and Achievement

2.2.3 Reviews Related to Achievement Motivation and Achievement

2.2.4 Reviews Related to Adjustment and Achievement

3. Methodology **54**

3.0. Introduction

3.1 Statement of the Problem

3.2 Selections and Classification of Variables

3.3 Hypotheses

3.4 Definition of the Terms

3.5 Tools Used for the Collection

3.6 Description of the Tools

3.6.1 Self-concept

3.6.2 Sinha's Manifesto Anxiety Scale

3.6.3 Deo-Mohan's Achievement Motivation Scale

3.6.4 Achievement Test

3.6.5 Adjustment Inventory and Scoring

3.7 Sampling

3.8 Statistical Technique Analysis of Variance (Anova)

4. Analysis and Interpretation of Data **93**

5. Summary and Conclusion **117**

5.1 Conclusions

5.2 Educational Implication

5.3 Scope of the Study

5.4 Limitations of The Study

5.5 Suggestions for Further Research

Bibliography **117**

Appendix **151**

Index **152**

Preface

Education is no longer a privilege. It is considered to be a birthright of every citizen in a civilized society, with the great progress made by science and technology and the complexities of modern life. Universal Education of a reasonably good quality has become imperative.

Physically Handicapped Children are one of the category of Exceptional Children and essential members of society. Their Handicapedness should not segregate them from normal children. They need some special training to develop themselves and to become a part of the society but not as a burden. This book deals with few factors to meet the requirement of PH children. They must develop self-concept Achievement motivation, unanxiety.

In addition to these, the subject matter of the book also has been thoroughly checked and revised to make a more readable and useful to its readers. It is therefore hoped that the book will serve the interest and purpose of readers in a more comprehensive and a useful way. The book is written in a lucid and an engaging style to assist the readers to grasp the subject better.

The book is dealing with the Exceptional Children, covers the major types of Exceptional children. Here the characteristics, means of identification, ethymology of their behavior along with their specific needs, problems, remedial education, provided in our country.

The book is organized into five Chapters. Chapter one deals with historical ground, concept, identification and characteristics of handicapped children. The second chapter deals with review of related literature. The third chapter deals with the methodology, hypothesis and statistical techniques involved. The fourth chapter includes analysis and interpretation of data. The fifth chapter gives the summary and conclusions of the study.

The author feels indebted to all those persons who with their writings and discussions have inspired her to bring out this book. Mr. Shreenivas Murthi, Mr. Joshi and Mr. Kumar deserve special thanks because it is their tireless efforts which has brought out the book well in time.

I am grateful to Shree Shamanur Shivashankarappa Hon'ble Secretary and other members of the BEA Association, Davengare. I have an incalculable depth of gratitude to my Lecturer who has guided me and helped to enrich my knowledge. I would like to express my special thanks to Vice-Chancellor Dr. Sayeda Akthar and Dr. Khajapeer, Dr. K. Chidananda Gowda and Dr. Shashidhar Prasad.

Finally, my sincere thanks to librarians, friends and family members and also to the Anmol Publications Pvt. Ltd., New Delhi.

—Dr. T.M. Geetha
Lecturer
Karnataka State Women University,
Bijapur

LIST OF TABLES

I.	Showing the population of disabled by age group and nature of disability in 1981	11
II.	Survey of persons with disability in Karnataka 1991 by disability type (Districtwise).	12
III.	Total population of disability with Percentage in Karnataka	13
IV.	Name of the schools and number of students selected for try out of achievement test.	73
V.	Criteria for selection of items based on index of discrimination	76
VI.	Difficulty level and index of discrimination of the items selected for achievement battery for IX standard	77
VII.	Number of items, time limit and marks allotted	81
VIII.	Number of students and schools, selected for the try out of adjustment inventory	84
IX.	Areas and the number of statements included in adjustment inventory for try out.	85
X.	Number of statements selected for adjustment inventory based on the chi- square value.	86
XI.	Areas and the number of statements included in the adjustment inventory for final administration	86
XII.	Name of the districts, school and number of students selected for the final administration.	88
XIII.	Number, mean and standard deviation of cells under different combination of independent variable self-concept, achievement motivation and adjustment.	94
XIV.	Summary table of analysis of variance of self-concept achievement motivation and adjustment.	94

XV.	Mean and standard deviation for the academic achievement scores of 2 levels of self- concept and anxiety groups.	95
XVI.	Summary table of analysis of variance for the achievement scores of 2 levels of Self-concept and anxiety groups..	96
XVII.	Mean and standard deviation for the academic achievement of scores of 2 Level of achievement motivation and self-concept.	99
XVIII.	Summary table of analysis of variance for the achievement scores of 2 levels of achievement motivation and self-concept groups.	100
XIX.	Mean and standard deviation for the academic achievement scores of 2 Levels of self-concept and adjustment groups.	103
XX.	Summary table of analysis of variance for the achievement scores of 2 levels of self-concept and adjustment groups.	103
XXI.	Mean and standard deviation for the academic achievement scores of 2 level of anxiety and achievement motivation.	106
XXII.	Summary table of analysis of variance for the achievement scores of 2 levels of anxiety and achievement motivation.	107
XXIII.	Mean and standard deviation for the academic achievement scores of 2 levels of anxiety and adjustment.	110
XXIV.	Summary table of analysis of variance for the achievement scores of 2 levels of anxiety and adjustment.	110
XXV.	Mean and standard deviation for the academic achievement scores of 2 levels of achievement motivation and adjustment.	113
XXVI.	Summary table of analysis of variance for the achievement scores of 2 levels of achievement motivation and adjustment.	114

1

Introduction

INTRODUCTION

School children are normally distributed into below average, average and above average. But there are a few children who may be found to deviate mentally, socially, educationally and physically from the normal children. These deviated children like other children, need security, love, affection, and satisfaction of their urges. When they are denied the satisfaction of their social and emotional needs, due to some reason or the other they become emotionally disturbed and suffer from adjustment problems. As result they fail to pay required attention to their studies and thus become educationally subnormal. Learning becomes futile, they become conscious of their inferiority complex and socially they feel isolated. There by, their achievement seems to be less when compared to normal children. Therefore they need careful attention. Such children distinctly require special educational care in a specialized manner. In addition to their problems especially in relation to the adjustments have to be considered. These deviated children are often designated as exceptional children. (Mathur 1962).

In education an exceptional child may be defined as one who differs so much from his peer average group in respect to physical, mental, or social characteristics so that he is unable to develop his fullest potential under normal conditions in the ordinary classroom for those some special organized schools have to be created. Exceptional children deviate significantly from the normal ones.

The deviation may fall either end for above the average or far below the average in one or more aspects of achievement. (Chintamanikar 1992).

Different persons have defined the word exceptional child; a few of them are discussed. According to Cruickshank (1967)."An exceptional child is one who deviates physically, intellectually, emotionally and socially so markedly from what is considered to be normal growth and development."

According to Baker (1965)., " An exceptional child is a child who is affected with a physical impairment that in any way limits preinhibits his participation in normal activities.

In the words of Kirk (1972), " The exceptional child is that child who deviates from the normal child in terms of their mental characteristics, sensory abilities, neuromuscular or physical characteristics, social and emotional behaviour, communication abilities, and multiple handicaps."

According to Barbe (1992), "Exceptional refers to those children who differ from the average to an extent that their differences need some type of special school adjustment."

Crow and Crow (1995) say that the term typical or exceptional is applied to a trait or to a person possessing the trait.

If the extent of deviation from normal possession of that is no great that because of it, the individual warrants and receives special attention from his behavioral responses and activities and thereby affected.'

Based on the above definitions the exceptional children are broadly classified into physically handicapped, mentally handicapped and the gifted.

Physically Handicapped Children

Physically handicapped children are one of the categories of exceptional children and essentially members of society, like others. A physically handicapped is that state of the body which obstructs the child from making normal progress in his school activities as average children do. (Different definitions and types of physically handicapped children are discussed while describing the concept of the physically handicapped children).

Mentally Handicapped Children

A child who is born mentally deficient or becomes so due to psychological and environmental factors is considered as a mentally handicapped child. They may also be termed as backward or mentally retarded.

The American Association of Mental Deficiency (AAMD) (Panda, 1997) refer to mental retardation as significantly sub-average in general intellectual functioning existing currently with deficits in adaptive behaviors and manifested during the developmental period. World Health Organization defines mental retardation as a condition of arrested or incomplete development of mind especially characterized by subnormality of intelligence. (Chintamanikar, 1994).

For educational purpose these children are divided into three distinct groups. They are 1) The Educable Mentally Retarded (EMR) who are found among pupils approximately in the I.Q. range 50 on the way to 75, it is impossible for them to be adequately educated in the regular classroom. They are capable of learning basic academic skills of reading, writing, and arthematics. They can also learn vocational skills. 2) The trainable or severely mentally retarded (TMR or SMR)who obtain I.Q. scores of approximately 30-50 they have very low intelligence as compared to E.M.R. They can learn reading and simple mathematics with much more effort. Their education is mainly based on various habits of daily life and training of skills. 3) The custodial or dependent mentally retarded (CMR or DMR). Who score below I.Q.-30. These children are not considered for school placement. It was assumed that all such children would be in residential institutions. (Dunn, 1964).

Gifted Children

The concept of giftedness varies widely. Havingrust (1992) defines the talented or gifted child is one who shows consistently remarkable performance in any worthwhile line of endeavor. (Chintamanikar).

The psychologists have defined giftedness on the basis of I.Q. Terman (1994) defined that children having an I.Q. of 140 and above are said to be gifted. 'These gifted children have superior cognitive ability, creativeness in thinking and superior talent in special areas."(Cruick shank, 1968). These gifted children can be placed in various categories such as having high mental ability, high educational achievement, high social talent, high mathematical ability and high artistic ability.

In order to develop these exceptional children to their maximum capacity, there is a need of modification in school practices or special education services is required. Because they are not able to receive classroom instruction in regular schools. This was the belief prevalent for several years. (Chintamanikar, 1992).

Many children are hard of hearing, but every such child is not exceptional unless the loss is such as to impair communication skills. Within particular group of exceptional children, there are also variations; there are different degrees of hearing loss. Hence it is appropriate to define exceptional children as those who differ from the average to such a degree in physical and psychological characteristics that the traditional school programmes does not allow all round development and progress for them.

Education Commission (1964-66) has suggested that the education of exceptional children is to be organized not merely on humanitarian grounds, but also on utilitarian ground proper education makes handicapped children enable to overcome their handicaps, and make them acceptable and useful citizens of the society and country at large. The commission also said that the primary objectives of education for the handicapped child should be to prepare him for adjusting in a socio-cultural environment. These children can also be educated by using special instructional methodology and instructional material and learning aids and equipments related to their learning needs. It also requires additional teaching competencies in general teacher and in some cases special teachers are indispensable, these needs have given rise to the component of education known as 'Special education'.

Special education according to Kaufman (1997) means specially designed instructions, which meet the unique needs of an exceptional child. It involves different types of teaching procedure, teaching content and equipment (use of ramps, hearing aids, crutches, wheel chairs and calipers etc.,) for a particular type of disability. In order to provide special education, the National Policy on Education in 1986 and as amended in 1992 also envisages special provision for the handicapped.

Exceptional children should receive a special education on account of the following reasons.

1. exceptional children do not get proper motivation in regular classroom work, as they need different treatment.

2. exceptional children may develop behavior problems if their specific needs are not properly attended to.
3. Principles of equality demands that all children must be provided equal opportunity so that they develop their potentialities to the maximum level.
4. education of the exceptional children will enable them to be self-supporting economically.
5. Several categories of children i.e., the deaf, the dumb, and the blind need different methods of teaching, instructional materials etc., which can be provided only in special schools.
6. Special education will train children to become useful productive members the society. (Agarwal 1995 & Kauffman 1994).

After briefly discussing, mentally handicapped children, we have discussed in detail the physically handicapped child in terms of the meaning, needs, and their education cohesions.

HISTORICAL BACKGROUND OF THE PHYSICALLY HANDICAPPED

Physically handicapped children come under the group of exceptional children. Throughout the ages, a child with a physical handicap has been a matter of concern to his family and to the society. In ancient times due to superstitions and ignorance such a child was believed to have been cursed by god or possessed by an evil spirit.

In ancient times the physically handicapped were either neglected or persecuted. A physically deformed child at birth in Sparta, for e.g., was left on the hills, or put in the great pit and also these children were often ridiculed in public and some of them employed as objects for the fun of noble men and kings. (Rohidekar and Usha, 1988)

In the middle ages, however, it became possible to divert some energy, care and money to the disabled. In Europe, medieval church became the social agency, which provided services to the disabled, which are today offered by public, private, welfare educational and health agencies. The amount of help available was however restricted due to the lack of information about health and educational problems. (Jaiswal, 1978).

In the early 14th century John Wallis and William Holders writing on the education of the deaf aroused the interest in Rousseau, regarding the special education of the handicapped and attempted to develop a positive trend in the attitude towards the physically handicapped during 18th centaury. (Jaiswal1978)

The expansion of education and the real programmes in special education was started in the 19 th centaury. In this period service to handicapped school children came into being. In the first decade of these centaury leaders such as Horace Mann, Howe and Doratheo Dix started a movement for the establishment of the residential schools for the physically handicapped. These schools provide protective environment for their entire life. (Hal Allen and Kaufman. (1994).

Today the emphasis on special education for the handicapped is increasing more and more. Specialized methods for helping such children to adjust to their needs are being evolved. (Rohidekar and Usha1988).

CONCEPT OF PHYSICALLY HANDICAPPED

Any physical or mental disability handicaps a child. Disability consists of impairment of structure and function; this can be either total or partial. For instance loss of vision of one eye or loss of hearing of one ear. But these impairment by themselves do not result in what we call handicap. A partially handicapped child is one who on account of injury, disease or congenital deformity, is substantially handicapped in studies or in undertaking work on his/ her own, which apart from the inquiry disease or deformity would be suited to his age, experience, and qualifications (Chintamaniker, 1992,and panda a, 1997).

Wright, (1960), World Health Organization (19760; Proposes a distinction between disability and handicap. Disability is a condition of impairment in physical or mental, impairment, having an objective aspect that can usually be described by a physician. A handicap is the cumulative result of the obstacles, which interferes between the individual and his maximum functional level of performance and activity. Therefore, physical impairment cannot be regarded as a psychological handicap.

According to Panda (1997,) the term handicap should not be regarded as a corollary to disability on the other hand it refers to disadvantage imposed by an impairment or disability upon a specific individual on his activities physical, mental, social, psychological and vocational etc,. The degree to which an individual is handicapped depends on the extent and nature of his physical and mental disability. It also depends upon the social definition of 'impairment', which means abnormalities of body structures and appearance of organ system, function resulting from any cause of physical impairment. An individual with colour blindness has impairment but it would be unlikely to lead to activity restriction. If his occupations were agriculture he might well be unaware of his impairment, but he would be at a disadvantage if he aspired to drive a railway engine. So the impairment, which constitutes the handicap, would depend on circumstances.

The terms physically handicap, disabled and crippled are used in an identical sense. (Chintamanikar, 1992)

[Harries and Head (1974)]; the definitions of handicap was summarized by Harries & head (1994) in the following salient points.

1. Handicap is the disadvantage or restriction of activity caused by the loss or reduction of functional ability.
2. The degree of handicap is the extent to which the activity is restricted.
3. The loss or reduction of functional ability depends not only on the type or impairment or the presence of disease, but on the ability to adapt, to minimize or to extend the effect of impairment.
4. The ability to adopt may be related to personality, intelligence, education, or encouragement received, encouragement could be positive as well as negative in that some relatives are over protective and never allow the person to try to adopt.

The definition of disabled proposed by United Nations aptly sums up what this study would like to characterize as a handicapped person. A person is unable to ensure by himself/herself, wholly or partly, the necessities of normal individual and social life, as a result of deficiency either congenital or not, in his or her physical or normal capabilities. (Mehta, 1983).

According to dictionary meaning a physically handicapped person is defined as possessing a physical defect which reduces one' efficiency in performing one's personal and social obligations according to a socially determined standard (Chintamanikar 19920. Educationally a child may be considered as handicapped if his/ her physical condition prevents full participation in childhood activities of social recreational, educational and vocational nature.

A physically handicapped child is one, who is affected with a physical impairment that in any way limits or inhibits his/ her participation in normal activities.

On accounts of this, the handicapped child has many problems in his/ her adequate adjustment. They are unable to participate in desirable, normal activities as normal children do. Their incapability develops some emotional problems like resentment and discouragement.

According to Bal Govind Tiwari,(1994). " Being handicapped too, and cannot avail of education they need special education and help. The handicapped of any part of the body leads to deviation in learning. Handicapped children differ in the limit and nature and their disability. A physical handicap is that state of the body which obstructs the child from making normal progress in his school activities as average does. They require special attention and equipment to control or overcome special disabilities.

Based on the above definitions, the physically handicapped children are classified as,

(a) The visually handicapped or blind.
(b) Acoustically handicapped or deaf.
(c) Speech handicapped or mute.
(d) Orthopaedically handicapped or crippled.
(e) Neurologically handicapped.
(f) Multi- handicapped.

Further handicaps can strike either at birth or at a later stage in the process of development. Those suffering from handicaps from birth may never know what normal living is, and as a consequence may suffer from less psychological disorders that accompany a handicap. Those who are striven by disability due to calamities after a long period of normal life find it extremely difficult to adjust.

Based on the National Sample Survey (N.S.S.). 1986, the researcher has quoted the statistics related to handicapped children's in India and Karnataka in particular.

TABLE-I (APPEN)

Population of Disabled by Age Groups and Nature of Disability in 1981

TABLE-1

Note: Based on prevalent rate given in nineteen and twenty eight of National sample Survey and total population in the population statistics paper 2 of 1983, series of India A.G. Office.

India

Out of 12 million disabled persons 2.6 million (1.21.H., 0.74 millions. SH, 0.53 millions. 0.12 millions. 10 percent have more than one handicap) fall in the age group 4-15 years. To this, should be added1.7 million MH children not covered in the survey of the disabled persons carried out by N.S.S.O. in 1986.The total disabled children falling in the UPE age group comes to 4.3 million.

Out of 1.4 million children fall in the age group 0-4 years which is relevant for identification, diagnosis, assessment, early stimulation and preparation for education. The disabled need education, and vocational rehabilitation subsequently are also to be considered.

On the basis of National sample surveys and (table1.1) other data are available. The ministry of HRD has made some tentative estimates of the number of physically handicapped children in the school going age in India. It is estimated that about 12.59 million children with disabilities are to be provided education in the school system. Out of which in the age group 5-14 children with disability 3.149 million, 1.48 million locomotors handicap, 0.65 million hearing handicapped, 0.91 million speech handicapped, 0.15 million visual handicap. Mentally retarded children 3.60 million, children with learning disability 3.60 millions children with disability with age group 16-18 years, 2.20 million. To this should be added 2 million disabled children in the age group 0-4 years.

Thus India may have blind, deaf and crippled children who ought to receive elementary education. It has not yet been possible to carry out even a sample survey for the enumeration of mentally handicapped children in India. But on the basis of surveys carried out in England and America (Which suggest that two to three out of every thousand children of school going age are mentally handicapped.) India would have about 10.39 million disabled children in the age group 6-14. At the present estimate of the population, therefore, a total provision for the education of about 10.39. Million handicapped children would have to be made in the country as a whole, if the directive of article 45 of the constitution is to be extended to handicapped children also. Further, the goal of universalisation of elementary education for this disadvantaged group would remain unachievable unless some urgent measures are taken.

TABLE –2 (APPEN)

Karnataka

The surveys identified a total number of 3., 55,819persons with disability in the Karnataka state. The distribution in detailed is given below.

TABLE III

Total Population of Disability with Percentage in Karnataka

	Type Persons	
1.	Visually handicapped	44,284 (12.44)
2.	Hearing Handicap	51,832 (14.56)
3.	Orthopaedically handicap Or Crippled	2, 04915 (57.58)
4.	Leprosy	10.662 (2.99)
5.	Mentally Retarded	36.850 (10.35)
6.	Multiple Disabled	7.276 (2.04)
	Total	3,55.819 (100.00)

The above table reveals, that more number (57.58%) of children are crippled. While children with multiple disabilities form the least (2.04%) other differences like mentally retarded, leprosy, visually impaired (12.44%). And hearing impaired (14.56%) are also found. it is very difficult to bring into normal as they require clinical approaches, whereas crippled children is subject to ratification through educational approaches, since other potentialities of the children are found to be normal. hence the researcher is concerned more on the crippled children, a detailed discussion about crippled child is presented in the pages to follow.

CONCEPTS, CHARACTERISTIC, AND IDENTIFICATION OF CRIPPLED CHILDREN

The present study was related to the crippled child. The problems of crippled children have been more than duly recognized these days. These children cannot adjust socially due to a crippled body. They are also categorized as being physically handicapped, lame and disfigured etc. Crippled children are less developed in physique than average children. They experience difficult ties in normal routine work. These children are weak due to malnutrition, sickness, paralysis, tuberculosis anemia, and other physical difficiencies. These children can be classified into two categories, the first often called the crippled or physical abnormality having muscular or skeletal deformalities which in many cases are apparent to the casual observe. They wear braces, or prosthetic devices such as artificial limbs or aid of crutches or wheel chairs. It includes children with cerebral palsy, poliomyelitis, osteomyelitis, muscular dystrophy and multiple sclerosis, clubfoot, epilepsy; the second category is abnormality due to sickness, which is not so radically recognized. They have a variety of chronic health ailments which confine them to bed for curtail their activity either periodically or chronically; crippled children are designated as the orthopaedically handicapped or the motor impairment (Mahesh Bhargava, 1994.)

One of the comprehensive definition is as follows.' A crippled means a condition of malnutrition, malfunction of loss of bones, muscles or body tissue which requires special education or related services,"(Mahesh Bhargava, 1994).

It can also be defined as follows. 'Crippled children are those who suffer from a defect that is accompanied by one or another type of deformity that inhibits the normal exercise of his/ her muscles joints or bones. (Chintamanikar1992)

State legislation often includes the child with cardiac disturbances or tuberculosis within the definition of crippled children. The crippled can be divided into two types the mild and the severe. The mildly crippled child as one who has problems like congenital anomalies such as dislocated hips or joint and the severely crippled is one who requires hospitalization on either temporary or permanent basis. (Chintamaniker, 1992).

This crippled nature is found in the children due to many causes. But a through knowledge of some main causative factors is necessary for planning a programme for them, the main factors are;

Hereditary Cause

Hereditary defect is one that passes down from generation, because of some sort of disturbance in the working of inherent gene mechanism. It is however note worthy that a particular condition may be hereditary and yet it may not manifest itself at birth or might not have appeared before in the individual's immediate family.

Congenital Cause

Congenital defect are those that are present at birth. Most common among congenital defects are clubfoot, dislocation of hips, missing bones, bowleg, webbed fingers. Etc,. Most of them are the result of infection, nutritional deficiency. Glandular disorder of the mother, maternal malnourishment, x-rays.

Acquired Cause

Acquired defects include birth, injury, accidents, nutrition deficiency defective bones or joints tumors and cancer. Any of the above causes may lead to the crippled- ness among children.

Characteristics of the Crippled Children

These crippled children are found to be different from those of the normal children in their characteristics some of them are discussed below. The crippled children possess the following characteristics.

They are passive, less persistent having shorter attention span. Engage themselves in less exploration and display less motivation. They are more dependent on adults, and interact less with peers. They have poor body image, high anxiety, and frustration. They are found to be quiet conforming, tender minded and somewhat tense. Area for Social relationships constitutes problem for many crippled youngsters. Their capacity for frustrations, tolerance, is lower than normal children. (Dykes1984; 85).

They possess a poor ego and unconscious guilt feelings and have a strong sense of fear. They often feel inferior. They are less creative than normal. They lack confidence in their abilities (Mathew1997).

Identification of the Crippled Children

The parents and the teachers must detect the crippling nature earlier at home and also in the school so that there will be change for a cure without permanent damage. The first step is to identify the child so that he can be referred for treatment. The teachers and parents must have in mind the following. Identification marks to recognize these children.

- Have poor motor control or co-ordination
- Walks with a limp or with awkwardness.
- Shows frequent pain in joints during exercise.
- Have jerking or shaky movements in walking.
- Amputed limbs.
- Difficulty in sitting, standing, and walking.
- Lack of control in all over the body, unable to co-ordinate the movement of two or three parts of the body. Ex. While plying, difficulty
- In moving hands and legs simultaneously or to bend the body in a particular direction.
- One or both feet turned downwards and outwards at ankle.
- Deviations in the running pattern- such as failure to alternate sides automatically, jerking, whipping, of the leg or the foot in or out is also observed.

- Lateral curvature of spine, body thrown out of alignment resulting in growth and deformalities.
- Deviations in standing or sitting patterns, such as weight shifted more to one side than the other or one part of the body twisted (e.g. The Trunk) with regard to the rate or the body.
- Loss of limb or extremities for one or the other reasons such as surgical operations, accidents etc.
- They fall frequently (Panda, 1997 et .at)

Apart from the above, the following identification may also be taken into consideration.

1. The teachers should go through the cumulative record to see if

   There is any evidence of a crippling disease for a specific child.
2. By conducting one-legged race i.e. ask the children to help a certain distance on the right foot and then return hopping on the left foot.
3. By conducting side ways race I, e, make the children to run sideways keeping their feet at right angles to the direction in which they are running (Reddy1997)

After the above testing if the teachers and parents found any remarks they may refer to those children to doctor or specialist for final identifications.

In conclusion, it can be said that this programme of identifying the physically handicapped children is beneficial for the schoolteachers especially at the elementary level. This programme also develops confidence in the teacher's powers of observation and a new perspective in a child in recognizing his potentialities and limitations in order to identify the handicaps.

ADJUSTMENT PROBLEMS OF THE CRIPPLED CHILDREN

Crippled children suffer from coping problems more than the normal children. It is because of one or the other type of organic defect. These defects influence their personality directly. Therefore these children are maladjusted. Adler (1927) while listing the types of person, who are likely to develop feeling of inferiority, had included prominently, the physically handicapped. Their disability affects their cognitive aspects, academic achievement, Intelligence, specific skills and interest (Mahesh Bhargav 1994). Body image theorists like Wilkins e.t. at. (1954), have demonstrated that children who depend more on others refluxed a lower evaluation or confidence in their own bodies, where as children who depend less on others have expressed more self- confidence. The knowledge of body image and its disruption due to chronic illness and physical disability constitute inferiority (Mc. Daniel 1969).

Earlier Studies on the Crippled Children (Drown et.at. 1988)

Have amply demonstrated that they suffered from feelings of inferiority, emotional imbalance, low level of school achievement and even inferior psycho- social development. They have also investigated that irrespective of type of handicap all the children suffering from adjustment problems revealed feeling of inferiority, loneliness, and depression. The disabled children are taken care at home and they are dependent. So loss of self-confidence unconscious fear neurotic attitude is more frequently found among them. They feel that they are different from others, incompetent and socially inadequate.

Thus when a crippled child is subjected to a teasing and torturing. It creates a situation where the child loses self-confidence and feels highly insecure. This makes him shy and timid, feeble mindedness, which results in scholastic backwardness and the consequent unsatisfying experiences in the class room, in turn, leads to truancy or other undesirable pursuits (Mahesh Bhargava, 1994). When the child is withdrawn from affection and security by teachers, parents, and associates, then it develops in him a feeling of being rejected and unwanted and parents do not understand him, do not find anything in the child except his short comings, punish him for slight offences, not helping him to do anything, not developing his interest not simulating him to self effort and thus encourage self reliance. This leads to a sense of personal worthlessness and the child feels lost and insecure and is prepared for anti- social sets.

In order to develop the good personality the child must adjust with the environment. If the adjustment is not proper it leads to the development of maladjustment and discontent. Normally the degree of adjustment depends partly upon the person's self-concept, Anxiety and achievement motivation. In addition they have to adjust with their own disabilities as well as to their social circle. Actually they have to bear a double burden such as social handicap and actual physical loss. (Agarwal, 1996).

In addition to these, the handicapped children have some of the other adjustment problems arising out of self-concept, Anxiety Achievement motivation and Adjustment. These are discussed in detail.

Self-Concept

According to the dictionary (Horace, 1965) meaning self-concept is nothing but a persons view of himself, the fullest description of himself of which a person is capable at given time (Definitions quoted by different persons are mentioned in the chapter page no. The concept of self has its origin in the pre- history of personality theory. The term self concept is used to refer to the organized cognitive structure derived from ones experience of his own self. The self- concept is a particular kind of attitudinal structure. It includes the elements of sheer perceptual recognition, which do not necessarily always correspond fully to the reality of the self. It also includes cognitive awareness of one's own behavior and interaction with other people and with the environment (Mc David e.t. at1968) a stable self-concept develops self-confidence, fearlessness, love and sympathy truthfulness, self-control etc. consequently the child will make better social adjustment and will enjoy greater social acceptance kundu (1989) Chauratru (1982) found that an integrated self- concept acts as a motivational force in maintaining mental health and influencing learning situations.

Self- concept is an image one holds of him self. It comprises of personal evaluation of one's characteristics, capacities aspirations and achievement and personal adjustment of an individual tends to be influenced by his self-concept Jerslid e.t. at. (1978) Indicated that self- concept is important in achievement because it affects the child's level of aspiration and self- expectations it is pointed out that a child who perceived himself unable makes him to be unsuccessful in his academic achievement.

Parameter (1970) suggested that the development of an adequate self-concept encourages the academic achievement. Moustaches (1970) suggest the following principles, which Summarize the basic approach and recognition of the self in true experience and the creation of human understanding.

(a) The individual knows himself better than any one side.

(b) Only the individual himself can develop his potentialities.

(c) The individual's perception of his own feelings, attitude and ideas is more valid than any outside diagnosis can be.

(d) The individuals' perception of him self determines how he behaves.

(e) As long as the individual accepts himself, he will continue to grow and develop his potentialities.

(f) The individual learns significantly only these things, which are involved in the maintenance of self.

David's and Greenberg (1967). Found that lower the level of self -esteem, lower is the level of achievement, while consequently higher levels of the self-concept were associated with higher level of achievement. Further high achievers were more able to express basic needs, suggesting that a stronger self-concept is associated with a greater willingness to risk self- experience an obvious requisite for achievement.

Children having poor opinion of themselves becomes self rejected they behave in a way that other regard as unsocial or immature, when they are not loved by their parents they become resentful, rebellious, negativistic and aggressive towards siblings whom they regard as the cause of parental rejection. When the self- concept is not developed properly, they lack individuality, which tends to make them self rejected.

Anxiety

Any situation that threatens the well being of the organism is assumed to produce a state of anxiety. According to dictionary meaning anxiety is an intense functional disturbance of the body that takes the place of conscious fear of anxiety (Horace, 1965). (Few more definitions were given in the chapter

111) Freud (1975) says that "anxiety is something felt unpleasant effect of state or conditions" This state was characterized by all that is covered by the word nervousness, apprehension, dread, frustration, depression etc. children should know their abilities and must have clear self-concept. Without the knowledge of these things they are maladjusted which gives rise to anxieties, worries, insecurity and tension. All these things are directly or indirectly come in the way of need satisfaction of the children (Hillgard, 1975,l, Munne, 1992). Threat physical disability. Threat to one's self- esteem and pressure to perform beyond one's capabilities produces anxiety. Frustration, of the basic needs develops anxiety. He tends to withdraw and to suppress or repress his feelings, he becomes moody. Normally anxiety arises in adjusting to the expectations and the standards of the school. If the family values are at variance with the values of the school. Then anxiety arises. A child who comes from homes where the cultural pattern is quite different from that of the teacher or the other students creates a difficulty in adjustment. Due to lack of personal attention at home, emotional disturbance are commonly found in children. Sometimes parents are unable to devote much individualized attention to each child. If the children feel deprived of their mother's love and attention then they are more likely to feel anxious. If the child's urges, desires or interests are frustrated, either because of lack of ability to satisfy them or because of unfavorable environment conditions, his emotional experiences follow a pattern of maladjustment (Lindgren, 1976)

Normally anxiety makes students receptive to learning. The lack of such anxiety in school situation makes the children careless of the right and feelings of others. Such children become self-centered. They do not care for others.

Children who suffer from over anxiety have difficulty in making progress in learning. They develop problems of behavior, which are undesirable. If a child appears in the examination with high anxiety, he is likely to mis- understood the questions and forgetting also results. Only the anxiety in the middle ranges stimulates the most effective learning.

Achievement Motivation

Motivation occupies a pivotal place in the process of teaching and learning. Achievement motivation is comparatively new concept in the world of motivation. According to Mc. McClelland et, at. (1953) Achievement has been defined as a concern for excellence in performance, as reflected in competition with the standards set by others or one self. Unique accomplishment or long-term involvement. According to Munn (1972) achievement motivation is defined as a desire for obtaining some specific standard of excellence. (Few more definitions were given in the chapter 111).

The children need motivation to learn for securing good marks in examination, when the child suffer from his disability he lacks his socializing behavior and also risk taking originality in expressing his own views. Lacks imitation, so he needs motivation. Motivation is an attracting others towards oneself, when he lacks motivation he will not be able to set some of standard for himself, so that he is pleased by his competence and disappointed with incompetence. (Heckhaucen. 1976). To achieve one's goal one needs to set aspirations at a higher level and try to overcome any obstacles to success. The basis of achievement motivation is achievement motive. Those who engage themselves in a task under the spirit of achievement motivation. The handicapped children those who posses les achievement motivation show the lower level of achievement. Where as the students with high achievement motivation show the higher level of achievement. Most of the students lack the opportunity to express their natural instincts, knowledge of goals and procedure, attitude of the teacher, lack of physical and environment condition, lack of appreciation, etc, to influence their performance different types of motivational techniques are to be employed to make them academically successful (Kaufman 1978).

Adjustment

As per dictionary meaning (Horracė 1965). Adjustment is a collection of harmonious relation to the environment where in, one is able to obtain satisfaction for most of the one's needs and to meet fairly well the demand, physical and social, put upon one (Few more definitions were given in chapter 111.) From he psychological point of view adjustment is the behavioral process by which human beings and other animals maintains equilibrium among their environment. These children deviate widely from thee average in certain traits. These deviations create certain problems of adjustment. These children do not take participation in activities common to the majority of other persons.

The term adjustment has two meanings in one sense; it is a continued process by which a person varies his behavior to a more harmonious relationship between himself and the environment. In other sense, adjustment is a state i.e. the condition of harmony arrived at by person whom we call well adjustment. (Parameshwar1988).

Due to their frustration, aggressive behavior will be developed instead of adjusting. When parents interfere with the wishes of their children they frequently turn upon them and express hatred and engage in some destructive, defiant or annoying behavior.

Too much of care, and protection of the parents towards these children damages the development. It deprives them of opportunities to learn. Things that other children of their age mates are learning. Failures to master the developmental tasks for their age means that they will make poor social adjustment and this will lead to poor personal adjustment.

Further children being frustrated in their attempts to learn to be independent the more they are frustrated, the more angry, resentful, and negativistic they become. Because parents often cannot understand their behavior feel that their children are unappreciative of all they have done for them, the parent child relationship deteriorate which creates a mal- adjustment (Elizabeth Hurlock, 1988).

Every child wants to be recognized and treated as individuals. As Eriksson has explained the search for identity a sense of being able to function as a separate person but with a close relationship to others. To be happy and well adjusted, children must have an inner assurance of their ability to function independently until they get this feeling of assurance, they are insecure, and failure to be recognized as individual is hazardous to good personal and social adjustment. Children who have self rejected attitude dislike themselves. And their playmates dislike them; they feel that they are not what they want to be. Quite a few children play truant from school because they find the school environment dull, monotonous and uninteresting. Rigid school organization, unwieldy classes. Uniform curriculum for all children, lack of pupil teacher contact encourages defeatism and embarrassment. If the child finds schools work beyond his power of assimilation, he runs away from the school and indulges in antisocial act. Such a child is also likely to be lazy disobedient, inattentive, quarrelsome, unstable and lonely. We can see two types of adjustment problems; conduct problems are of two types (1). Problems of limited social significance and (2). Problems of serious social significance. Those of limited social significance, are particularly associated with home include feeling difficulties, insomnia, grinding of teeth, thumb sucking, nail biting, disobedience stubbornness, incompatibility with parents and sibling, difficulty in making friends others of serious social significance are of fundamentally anti-social in nature and all types of delinquencies such as steeling, truancy, begging, gambling, cruelty, homicide and suicide.

Personality problems include aggressiveness, submissiveness or withdrawing behavior, which manifests itself in various forms such as inferiority feeling, shyness, and exclusiveness hypersensitivity absentmindedness. Secretiveness and feelings of being persecuted. All these behavior problems make adequate adjustment rather difficult; personality problems of the most serious type include psychoneurosis and psychoses, which make adequate adjustment nearly impossible.

EDUCATION OF THE EXCEPTIONAL CHILDREN

The nature of the exceptional child is hereby explained by integrating the views of experts like Cruickshank, Fleming, Kirk and Crow, ' As exceptional child is he who markedly deviates in physical, mental social, educational, emotional and behavioral characteristics to such an extent that he requires a modification in a routine class room teaching or needs the specific teaching methods and programs that he may develop his abilities, capacities and potentialities to the maximum. So even in a normal class, they can be given special education by special visiting teachers, social workers, and specialties in handling various handicaps. These people may provide assistance to parents and teachers in understanding exceptional children in educating and guiding them by visiting the school from time to time.

The primary responsibility in this method of education lies with the class teacher in training exceptional child but he gets, help from these special persons also at times to help the child to develop his abilities and make proper adjustments. This type of arrangements is useful in those schools and areas, where the number of exceptional children is less or the status of exceptionality is very low. By classifying exceptional children according to their specific needs. Extra class planning can be done in normal classes. So that the exceptional child gets proper guidance, training and education according to his special needs this is important for emotional and social adjustment of these exceptional children. This is important for emotional and social adjustment of these exceptional children. When the performance levels of exceptional children are too low to adjust with the normal children of the class. Under such conditions special class planning becomes absolutely essential. The success and effectiveness depends upon the efficiency of the specially trained teacher. Subject experts and guides give training and vocational guidance to their children in these classes with the help of the specially required material and techniques (Mahesh Bhargava)

These exceptional children can also take education in special schools but is very important to fulfill the needs and development of exceptional children by making provisions for special schools. Special classes and buildings are constructed in these schools and adequately trained, able teachers, doctor, and directors are to be appointed who can give both formal and informal education through special tools and instruments. It can be more useful to train them in ant profession according to their specialties also. By proper co- ordination between parents, social workers, teachers and administrators such arrangements can be done to the best use for the benefit of these exceptional children. (Agarwal, 1995,).

Establishment of the residential schools. Fulfill the necessities of those children who require special training for a prolonged period because of their exceptionalities. In order to develop socially, physically and emotionally, physical education is to be provided. It also helps in the development of perceptual motor abilities such as balance, literality, body image, spatial awareness, strengthens the muscle and cardiovascular endurance, flexibility and motor co- ordination. The regular sports activities should be suitably modified to suit to the capabilities of the disabled. Play and sports for the disabled should be more organized and structured than those of the normal child. (Panda, 1997).

EDUCATION OF THE CRIPPLED CHILDREN

Remarkable progress has been made during recent years for the education of the crippled children. In the metropolitan cities of India, many schools have incorporated many unusual features including medical and therapeutic equipments to meet with the educational and physical needs of these children. These crippled children are always like the normal children except for their physical deformity. Though they cannot do physical work with so much efficiency, their desires and ambitions are like those of normal children. They require such education, which is in tune with their physical fitness. The education of the crippled children should be extensive so that their whole personality can be developed. The schools may take following steps to provide better provisions to their children.

Social and emotional adjustment is badly affected to physical abnormality. Therefore their emotional adjustment should be taken care of, we have to make such activities and such a school organizational atmosphere through which their inferiority complex can be removed, and a feeling of self-confidence, and self-direction can be aroused within them. The teacher should not be harsh; they should be patient and sympathetic towards the expression of children's emotions. He should sublimate the emotions of children by presenting suitable opportunities and situation for their healthy expression. Scientific method of teaching and existence of co-curricular activities would promote the emotional development of the child of ethics, standards and ideals of society leads to emotional disturbance, so it must be avoided. Thus education and teachers are the two great factors to modify the emotions of children and prepare them for a well-composed and balanced life. As far as possible vocational training should be given to these children. This may develop physical efficiency in them.

Motivation and Determination

Teacher should motivate these children in a manner by which self-determination can be promoted, which may enable them to fulfill the aims of education and life. (Motivation techniques were discussed in the v chapter.)

Medical Aids

By giving medical aid and therapy, these crippled children can be made healthy, so that they become successful in getting educational and vocational training. Education of the crippled children has changed considerably over the past 50 years, due to the concerned and involvement of the society. These crippled children can be integrated in regular classroom where convenient hand nails, ramps, wide doors, no doorsills and attendance in classroom are facilitated. Special classrooms are to be located in the ground floor normally for those orthopedic disabilities where special equipments are provided. e.g. Standing tables, parallel bars, relaxation chairs.

In addition to the above physical facilities, other facilities may be provided in schools such as

1. Construct a short ramp on steps to enable children in wheel chairs or crutches to enter the building.
2. Addition of hand bar by the side of a water tap, in a toilet, or near a section of the blackboard.
3. Desks should be removed to make room for the wheel chair to move.

4. Adjusting seats to turn to sides so that the child with braces can sit more easily.
5. Rubber mats over slippery sections of the floor within the classroom.

In the education of these crippled children with motor handicaps premium is placed on intellectual development, academic ability, and facilitating the child's total adjustment to limitations.

1. These children should be taught self-reliance, initiative and the ability to make choices. They must learn to plan ahead for mobility and assistance.
2. They should be taught how to use different parts of the body.
3. Teachers were ought to see that they develop workable self-concept. Those children should play by mixing with their non-handicapped peers.
4. The school must develop creativity in the children with reference to art, rhythm, music, and drama
5. Teacher's praise and acceptance are significant by help for improving personal development.

GENESIS OF THE PROBLEM

The problem of adjustment of crippled children has been a basic interest, not only to educational but also to sociologists and physiologists. The subjects have received much significance, in these days.

Every society has a social responsibility to provide compulsory schooling for all children of a defined age groups (-.14). It is important to identify and provide opportunities for the development of the full potentialities of every child. In this process when the efforts are inadequate, the academic achievement, which is an end product, will be less. Children are the backbone of every society and play an important role in its scientific and technological development. But crippled child hinder in its own development and societal development.

It is of prime importance to know why some children achieve high while others achieve low in the same school environment. Terman (1974) pointed out that intelligence and achievement is far from perfect correlation. Much remains to be discovered as to why some children fails to use their intelligence, there must be certain aspects of the personality which reinforce and further the pursuit of academic goals.

A few researchers have been done in relation to the academic achievement of the handicapped children by taking a few factors like age, socio-economic-status, intelligence, aspirations, self- concept motivation Singh (1983) Gyani, (1984) Mathur Abba (1985) The researcher has not come across any studies related to crippled children to show the effect of different levels of self-concept, anxiety, achievement motivation and adjustment on academic achievement and also to show that whether the interaction between the two factors have any impact on achievement or not.

One of the reasons for lack of research in this area is, because they could see and hear, they did not attract the special attention of the public in respect of education till about the middle of the 20th centaury. And also there is a very little involvement of the universities and dearth of persons who can carry out and supervise in this area.

It has prompted the researcher to make an attempt to study the impact of levels of self- concept, anxiety, achievement motivation and adjustment problems of the handicapped children in relation to their academic achievement.

The researcher being a teacher educator found that the provisions made for these physically handicapped children is meagree; schools have not developed infrastructure facilities to meet the special needs of these unfortunate members of the society.

The purpose is to help the child and the teacher to identify and concentrate on the above factors, which help them to improve their achievement. Efforts have, however, been made in India to study the problems of physically handicapped in the field of sociology, psychology and social work. But still studies in this area, particularly in Karnataka re wanting. The orthopaedically handicapped in this study includes the lame (deformed in either one or both of the legs). Or crippled (deformed in the muscles and joints). Only a small proportion of crippled children suffer from mild defects, which could be rectified earlier. But by negligence of the parents the original deformity multiplies as a result of which the child becomes seriously crippled. The two great crippling diseases are poliomyelitis and infantile paralysis and tuberculosis of bones and the joints.

The study is limited only to the crippled children of the age group 6-14. It does not take into account other categories of the physically handicapped children.

STATEMENT OF THE PROBLEM

The problem taken up for investigations can be stated in precise terms as' Study of the adjustment problems of handicapped children of secondary schools, in relation to the academic achievement in Karnataka state with reference to Chitradurga, Dharwad, and Bellary district "

NEED AND IMPORTANCE OF THE STUDY

In India, research on education of orthopaedically handicapped has not received the attention it deserves. It is only recently that some attention is being paid. It is through education that researcher can bring about some changes for the better. Education of the handicapped has national significance also. Hence, there is the need to provide education suited to them. it will help to prevent, reduce or eliminate the problem in the fields of academics, communications, locomotors, and adjustment of orthopaedically handicapped children.

The preamble of the constitution states that justice, liberty, equality and fraternity should be secured to the citizens of India. All these will have no meaning if they are not provided facilities for education, which is one of the fundamental rights, that is, education for all. If this facility is not provided social economic and political development is not possible. Article 45 of the constitution directs that free and compulsory education should be provided for all children until they complete the age of 14 years irrespectively of their handicap ness.

The orthopaedically handicapped pupils are just normal children except foe their physical deformity, therefore it is necessary to provide special facilities in addition to the facilities provided in normal children The education for orthopaedically handicapped is important for the development of the country and also to build up the needed resources. In our constitution a few provisions have been made for their education, which have to be followed up with right spirit and perspective. However, there is paucity of research in this area. This may be perhaps that this area has not attracted the attention of the researchers. Hence here is a need for research in the education provided to these children, which might delimits information required to revitalize the educational programmes.

The present study is an attempt to study the performance of orthopaedically handicapped children in respect to their adjustment problems.

OBJECTIVES OF THE STUDY

This study has been undertaken with the following objectives which are intended to assess the:

1. Academic achievement of physically handicapped children of high and low self-concept group.
2. Academic achievement of physically handicapped children of high and low anxiety group.
3. Significance in the interaction between self concept and anxiety on academic achievement
4. Academic achievement of the physically handicapped children of high and low achievement motivation group.
5. Academic achievement of physically handicapped children of high and low self-concept group.
6. Significance in the interaction between achievement motivation and self-concept on academic achievement
7. Academic achievement of physically handicapped children of high and low adjustment group.
8. Academic achievement of physically handicapped children of high and low anxiety group.
9. Significance in the interaction between adjustment and self-concept on academic achievement.
10. Academic achievement of physically handicapped children of high and low anxiety group.
11. Academic achievement of physically handicapped children of high and low achievement motivation group.
12. Significance in the interaction between anxiety and achievement motivation on academic achievement.
13. Academic achievement of physically handicapped

children of high and low anxiety group.

14. Academic achievement of physically handicapped children of high and low adjustment group.
15. Significance in the interaction between anxiety and adjustment on academic achievement.
16. Academic achievement of physically handicapped children of high and low achievement motivation group.
17. Academic achievement of physically handicapped children of high and low adjustment group.
18. Significance in the interaction between achievement motivation and adjustment on academic achievement.
19. To construct an adjustment inventory to identify their adjustment.
20. To construct an achievement test to measure their achievement.

AN OVERVIEW OF THE STUDY

Chapter 1 deals with the introduction of exceptional children, historical background of the physically handicapped children, concept of physically handicapped, survey report, concept of orthopaedically handicapped. Adjustment problems of orthopaedically, handicapped genesis of the study, statement of the problem, objectives of the study and as overview of the study.

In chapter 2 a brief review of related literature and how the related literature helped the researcher to design the present study is discussed. For better understanding the related literature reviewed by the researcher will be classified as studies related to:

1. Self-concept and academic achievement

2. Anxiety and academic achievement
3. Achievement motivation and academic achievement
4. Adjustment and academic achievement.

In chapter 3, methodology used in the present study is discussed. This chapter includes restatement of the problem. Selection of variables, definitions of the term, formulations of the hypothesis, sampling procedure. Description and justification of selected tools for collection of data, administration and scoring procedure and finally a brief description of various statistical tools used for the analysis of data and justification in selecting them will be discussed.

Chapter 4 deals with the analysis, presentation and interpretation of data.

Chapter 5 presents a brief summary of all the chapter, it also present conclusion drawn on the basis of interpretation, educational implications, the limitations of the study and suggestions for further research.

2

Review of Related Literature

INTRODUCTION

In the previous chapter, concept of orthopaedically handicapped children, characteristics, and identification of crippled children. Adjustment problem of the crippled children, statement of the problem have been dealt with. In this chapter a brief review of studies related to self-concept, Anxiety, Achievement motivation and Adjustment and their relation to Academic achievement has been discussed.

IMPORTANCE OF REVIEW OF RELATED LITERATURE

To understand the reason for presenting the review of related literature, it would be worthwhile to consider its importance.

1. It provides the researcher the means of getting to the frontier in her particular fields of knowledge.
2. It helps to understand the theory in the field and gives knowledge with regard to the procedure and tools, which are proved.
3. It avoids unintentional duplication of previous studies and keeps the researcher in a better position to interpret the significance of her own results.
4. It assures familiarity with both previous theory and research in the researcher. (Donald Ary 1972).

According to Borg (19989) "The literature in any field forms the foundation upon which all future work will be built. If we feel to build the foundation of knowledge provided by the review of related literature one work is likely to be shallow and native and will often duplicate work that has already have done better by some one else.

In the words of John Best (1992), 'The review of related literature is a valuable guide to define the problem, recognizing its significance suggesting, promising, data gathering devices, appropriate study design and sources of data.

Thus it could be seen that the review of related literature is a very important and essential step in designing any research work. At the same time the richness of source material in the development of a research design depend not so much on the area covered by the previous researcher in the field but on the specificity of significance studies around a few crucial variables.

Hence review of related literature becomes imperative on the part of the researcher to review of the work done by other researchers. The related literature obtained is more in connection with the visually and other impairment excluding crippled, because this area has not attracted the attention of researchers in our country. Hence, it is essential to know about the studies conducted in relation to the self-concept, anxiety, achievement motivation and adjustment of the physically handicapped children.

The researcher could get very few reviews on the subject. Therefore, the studies reviewed by the researcher were classified into four categories as studies related to

1. Self-concept and academic achievement
2. Anxiety and academic achievement
3. Achievement motivation and academic achievement

4. Adjustment and academic achievement of handicapped children.

CORRELATES OF ACHIEVEMENT

Reviews Related to Self-Concept and Academic Achievement

Studies that have been conducted to identify the relationship between self-concept and academic achievement have been reviewed here.

Deo Pratibha and Sharma Sagar (1970) studied the effect of self-concept on academic achievement. Their sample consisted of 700 students of which 362 boys and 388 girls studying in the final years of higher secondary school of 4 states.

Methodology and instrument; self-concept, inventory based on Deo's personality word list which was standardized by Sharma, was used Marks obtained in Punjab University higher secondary examination were taken as achievement. Using SDS Kurtosis and Shewner made data analysis. The self-concept scores and achievement scores were calculated. Coefficient of correlation was calculated between the two sets of scores and it was found to be non-significant. The significance of the differences between self-concept groups was tested by using critical ratios.

Results; the group having middle level of self-concept had scores of high achievement than those who had very high or very low self- concept. The students with low self-concept and high self- concept differed significantly from the middle group but did not differ among themselves in achievement. A student with high self-concept performs better than those with low self- concept.

Swami; GO (1978), worked on the study of the self-concept of the adolescence and their relationship with scholastic achievement and adjustment.

The objectives of the investigations were (1) To study the nature of the distribution of self-concept of adolescents.(2) To study the self-concept of adolescents in relation to sex, intelligence and place of residence. (3) To find out the relationship between self-concept and scholastic achievement. (4) To find out the relationship between self- concept and adjustment. (5) To construct a test on self-concept.

The descriptive method of research was followed to carry out the study.

The findings of the investigation were: 1) It seemed that the male adolescents received more encouragement and attention at home and in society than the female. (2) The more intelligent adolescents tended to have brighter self-concept than the less intelligent one's. (3.) There existed a positive relationship self-concept and achievement. The adolescents with good self-concept were likely to achieve more than those with poor self-concept. (4) Scholastic achievement is highly correlated with the concept ones' mental health, and SES, (5) Their exists a strong relationship between self-concept and adjustment.

Sara Swat (1982) studied the self-concept in relation to the adjustment, values of academic achievement, socio-economic status and sex of high school students of Delhi.

The main objectives of the study were to examine the relationship of self-concept measures with adjustment, values, academic achievement and S.E.S. of boys and girls.

A random sample of 840 students (420 boys and 420 girls0 of class IX from 14 schools under the Delhi administration was selected. Data were collected by using the self-concept inventory developed by the researcher the Vyaktitva Pareeksha

Prashnvali by Saxena and the study of values by Ojha. The achievement was measured by obtaining annual examination marks of the previous classes. Adjustment was measured by Kulshreshta. Product moment correlation, t-test, multiple regression analysis and coefficient of multiple determinants were used to analyze the data.

The major findings were: (1) The boy's self-concept was positively and significantly related to social adjustment, while the girls self-concept was positively and significantly related to home, health, social emotional, school as well as total adjustment. (2) The boy's self–concept was positively and significantly related and religious values, while the girls self-concept was not related to any of these values. (3) Only intellectual self-concept was positively and significantly related to academic achievement in both the sexes. (4) Boys and girls differed significantly on total self-concept and its physical, social, and moral dimensions, were considered. Girls were found to be higher in all these dimensions.

Harvey, Davis, Greenway, Philip (1982) worked on parent attitudes and emotional reactions affecting their handicapped child's self-concept.

He investigated the relationship between parental attitude and the handicapped child's self esteem with 24 physically handicapped children with normal intelligence aged 9-11 years. Parents who were close together in their primary mood reactions had the most influence on their child's self-esteem, and mother who confronted the handicapped and came to terms with it were those whose children had higher self-esteem.

Michel (1983) studied the self concept of the mild handicapped and the role of social comparison. He tested the hypotheses derived from social comparison theory by assessing their self-concepts of different groups among elementary school children. He administered the piers- Harries- children's self-concept scale. In the first contrast handicapped students were found comparable in self-concept to normal students 2nd prediction found a strong support that lower self-concept should be clearly evident when children are forced to reside solely social comparisons group of generally greater ability. The final hypothesis suggests that higher self-concept for handicapped students are partially segregated from the larger school population rather than totally.

Timberlake, Elizabeth (1985) worked on self-concept protection by children with physical differences. Finding shows that 85% of the students who were also experiencing academic difficulty, used defensive adaptive techniques several times a week to protect their sense of self and self-work from a mental representation of body image as different or defective. Significant differences in coping style were identified between the 10 students who acquired these differences later. Members of the first group were likely to use defensive adaptive techniques designed to repair the difference symbolically (e.g. identification, compensation) while members of the later groups were likely to use defensive adaptive techniques designed to eradicate the physical difference.

Weller, Roger, Truex, Wayne (1985) worked on assessing the effects of experimental studies on the self- concept of the pre-adolescent physically handicapped. He divided the students as control group and experimental group. For both the groups he has given a therapeutic treatment and the treatment of passive stimulation. Child profiles, which (J.B. Geier and D.E. Downey 1979) assess how children see themselves and what they think is expected of them.

Results indicate that students maintained a positive self-concept throughout the study and in no way the participation in the project affected them negatively.

Super, John-Block (1992) studied the self-concept and need for achievement of men with physical disabilities. Studied self-concept and need for achievement of athletically active and relatively inactive. American males with physical disabilities using the Tennessee self-concept scale, counseling form, Thematic Apperception Test. Subjects were 45 men with physical disabilities and 50 able-bodied were also included. Results predicted negligible differences between the disabled students and the able bodied.

Hessian (1988) attempted to study the effect of self-concept on levels of academic achievement and school backgrounds.

The samples of the study consisted of 180 students who were selected randomly from class XI of government. Private and public schools of Pithoragarh and Nainital cities of Uttar Pradesh. The high school marks were taken as the criterion of academic achievement. Mohsin's (1979) self-concept inventory was used to measure the self –concept of the students. The conclusions of the study were (1). Academic achievement is relatively related with self-concept. (2) High academic achievers, because of their preoccupations in studies, do not have much concern with and their image of themselves. (3) Types of school background influence the self–concept of students in a significant way.

Jain and Pandit (1990) studied self-concept and identification of academic goals. The objectives of the study were to know whether the self-concept has a bearing on the identification of academic goals of adolescent girls.

The study consisted of a sample of 520 girls studying in IX and X grades selected randomly from 40 high schools situated in Nagpur City. Self-concept test constructed by Goswami and et. al. (1979) was administered to measure self-concept. Academic goals of the subjects were assessed from their responses to a fact of the identification tool. The conclusion of the study was, the adolescent girls with high self-concept tented to have higher academic goals.

Reviews Related to Anxiety and Achievement

Studies that have been conducted to identify the relationships between Anxiety and Achievement have been reviewed here.

Agarwal, Rita, Kaur, Jasbir, (1985) studied on the anxiety and adjustment levels among the visually and hearing impaired and their relationships to locus of control, social, cognitive, and biological variable.

Studied the personality dynamics of 45 hearing impaired and 40 visually impaired residential school children (6-16 years) to examine the relationships between stress and stresses. Students were administered measures of adjusting anxiety, and locus of control, scores relating to intelligence and academic level teacher and peer acceptance, and biographical variables were also obtained. Findings show that the correlation between anxiety and adjustment differed qualitatively as well as quantitatively between the groups.

Wilhelm, James (1989) worked on fear and anxiety in low vision and totally blind children. He conducted a survey on fear and administered a manifest anxiety scale, for 139 visually impaired children. Students were classified into totally blind and low vision groups. Fears and anxiety scores of totally blind students were similar to those of low vision students. General levels of anxiety for the total sample compared favourably with the general population. Students fear tented to reflect concern for bodily injury.

Hasnain, Metha, Joshi, (1982) worked on the self-disclosure, anxiety and ascendance submission anxiety among physically handicapped and normal students.

He compared 10 handicapped and 10 normal students on their responses to self-disclosure. An inventory, a comprehensive response to self-disclosure, inventory submission scale was given to the students. Results show that normal student self-disclosure was significantly more than handicapped students. A slight difference was found in the anxiety scores of normal and handicapped students. Handicapped students were significantly more ascendant and submissive than normal children.

Jones Reginald (1974) studied on the correlates of orthopaedically disabled children school achievement and interpersonal relationships. The study attempts to correlate the orthopaedically handicapped children's school achievement and interpersonal relationship. Results indicate that there is a full range of achievement. Rated physically dependency was statistically independent of achievement.

Murphy Harry (1 976) worked on the comparative studies of academic achievement between hearing and non- hearing-impaired students of California State University.

Studied the academic achievement between hearing impaired and non–hearing-impaired students. He found that the academic achievement of non-hearing-impaired students at California University is significantly superior at each class level to that of hearing impaired students.

Pliner, Susan, Hannah, Mary E. (1985) studied the role of achievement that teacher hold negative attitude (as indicated by placement in more restrictive environment) towards this group only when the child's level of achievement is low. When achievement was at an acceptable level, teachers were positive towards the handicapped.

Smith, Karl, Johnsonroger (1982) worked on the effects of cooperative individualistic instruction on the achievement of handicapped, regular and gifted students. Results indicate that cooperative learning experiences promoted higher achievement, greater retention, more positive attitude and higher self-esteem than did individualistic learning experience.

Pamapriya, Mythili (1988) worked on the comparative study of deaf and normal children cognitive factors and academic achievement, they selected 52 deaf & 52 normal children for the study (11-18 years). He used Raven's standard progressive matrices and a paired associate list as measures of intelligence learning and recall. Academic Achievement was determined by taking the average of annual examination marks of 2 recent years for each 5 students. Results show that deaf students were significantly less intelligent and recalled significantly less number of visual imaginary words and auditory imaginary words than normal students. Findings showed a significant relationship between intelligence, learning and recall and academic achievement for normal students and for deaf students, only auditory imaginary and total on trial were significantly related to academic achievement.

Mavor-in-Cavour-Jana, Levandoswal (1986) studied on the comparison of the attitudes of mother of non-handicapped children and of mentally retarded children towards their child and their relation to school behaviour.

He examined the relationship between children behavior at school and their mother attitude towards them. He interviewed with 357 mothers of non-handicapped children, and 93 mothers of mildly retarded children. In the non-handicapped children emotional components of the mothers attitude were associated with assessment of children academic achievement, while motivational components were associated with assessment of general behavior. For the handicapped children the relationship between school behavior and maternal attitude was less clear. Maternal attitude towards these children were less related to academic achievement.

Reviews Related to Achievement Motivation and Academic

Studies that have been conducted to identify the relationship between achievement motivation and academic achievement, have been reviewed here.

Michael (1974) studied on the relationship between maternal reinforcement and help, and the achievement motive in normal hearing and hearing impaired sons.

Correlated the observed behaviors of 64 mother helping their sons to perform 2 verbal and 2 nonverbal tasks with the autonomous and social comparison achievement motive scores for 31 hearing impaired boys and 33 normal hearing boys. Autonomous Achievement scores were positively related to non-specific direction for the hearing impaired the directions of the relationship between autonomous achievement motive scores and reward was different for each of the 2 groups for the verbal tasks the normal hearing children had higher social comparisons. Achievement motive scores than did the hearing impaired.

Andreanska, Viasa, Andreanska, Misrosla (1981) studied on the specificities of motivation in handicapped children. It is reported that a) Contrary to the normal population, the sequence of their motivation responses was contingent on the type of activity to be performed and thus was not a stable personality characteristic as has been found. b). There are differences in the motivational behaviors of individuals with different handicaps. In the mentally retarded for example external stimuli were more effective motivational one than the internal stimuli.

Bharathi (1984) studied the self-concept and Achievement motivation of early adolescents.

The objectives of the study were. To study 1) the aspects

of self-concept, that is real, ideal self-concept and self-ideal discrepancy. 2) To observe the interaction effects of age, sex, and socioeconomic status and achievement motivation.

The tools used in the study were (i), the Rao Socio Economic Status Scale (1973). 2). The Mehta Achievement Motivation Test for high school boys. (1969),(3). The Self-concept Inventory with two dimensions real self–concept and ideal self-concept the last tool measures four aspects viz. ability adjustment, personal social orientation, masculinity and feminity. The split half reliability was 0.86 and it had content validity.

Findings seem that no age differences were found in self-concept with respect to adjustment, no sex differences were found to be the highest among the high SES groups and lowest in low SES groups.

Chaterji (1983) worked on a comparative study of personality, intelligence and achievement motivation of students in different academic groups.

Finding seems that 1. Science students were significantly higher in achievement motivation in comparison with other groups. 2. Scores on intelligence test in science and commerce groups were significantly higher than those of all other groups. 3. Scores on achievement motivation of students of science or commerce were significantly higher than those of the other groups.

Indrani (1985) conducted a study on relationship between academic achievement and achievement motivation of the 9th standard students.

The major finding was (1) There is a significant high positive relationship between academic achievement and achievement motivation. (2) There is a significant positive relationship between academic motivations on total scores.

Mamatha (1992) worked on the correlative study of achievement motivation in relation to self-concept, adjustment problems and SES in IX std, students of Bangalore city.

1. To find out the level of achievement motivation in 9th std students.
2. To find out the relationship between achievement motivation and self-concept of the 9th std students.
3. To find out the relationship between achievement motivation and adjustment problems.
4. To find out the combined effect of self–concept adjustment problems and Socio-economic status in relation to achievement motivation of students studying in 9th std. The size of the sample consisted of 184 students. The tools used were Worthy's self-concept scale, Bells adjustment, Kuppuswamy's revised SES scale. Prayag Mehta's Achievement Motivation inventory, to test the hypothesis product moment correlation and multiple correlations was used.

Findings seem that 1. There is a very low and negative correlation between achievement motivation and adjustment problems of students. 2. The relationships between achievement motivation and self-concept combined with adjustment problem among the students studying in government school are very high.

3. The relationship between achievement motivation and self-concept is very high.

Reviews Related to Adjustment and Achievement

Studies that have been conducted to identify the relationship between adjustment and achievement have been reviewed here.

Singh (1983) studied on the pattern, achievement and adjustment of mentally superior children, the objectives were 1). To study and compare the need pattern of mentally superior children with those of average children. 2. To study and compare with their I.Q. & 3. To study and compare the adjustment in social, health, home, emotional and sexual areas of superior children with those of average children. The adjustment inventory by Singh and Singh and Indian adoption of Rotter and Raffertys incomplete sentence blank for measuring adjustment in social and sexual areas. The achievement scores were taken from the annual examination marks. The data were analyzed with the help of correlation technique.

Pandey (1985) studied on the affectional deprivation, ego, strength, and adjustment pattern among visually handicapped children and their relationship.

The major objective of the study was to make a psychological study and affectional deprivation, ego, strength and adjustment among visually handicapped children and their rehabilitation.

The tools used by him for adjustment was Adjustment inventory by Eysenck's; Maudsley personality inventories (M.P.I. Jalota Kappor (1965). Findings seems that; 1. The deprivation as felt by rural blind children was significantly more acute than that felt by urban blind children.2. There was no significant difference in the pattern of affectional deprivation between congenitally blind children and post nately blind children.

Mathur, Abha (1985) worked on the comparative study of the adjustment problems, level of aspirations, self-concept and academic achievement of crippled children and normal children; he did a comparative study on crippled and non-crippled children.

Objectives of the study were: 1. To compare the home adjustment, health adjustment, social adjustment, emotional adjustment, school adjustment and total adjustment of crippled and normal children. 2. to compare the level of aspirations of crippled and non-crippled children. 3. To compare the self-concept of crippled and non-crippled children. 4. To compare the academic achievement of crippled and non-crippled children.

The sample comprised of 50 crippled and 50 non-crippled children ranging in age from 13 years to 16 years studying in high schools.

The tools used were 1. General mental ability test by Jalota.2. Vyaktitva Pareeksha Prashnavali by Saxena.3. Self-concept inventory by Singh.

Findings of the study were: 1. Crippled children differed significantly from normal children in all types of adjustment.2. Crippled boys differed significantly in social adjustment while crippled girls differed significantly from normal girl's social adjustment.Emotional, adjustment and total adjustment. 3. Significant differences were found between crippled and non-crippled in the level of aspiration measured in terms of goal discrepancy scores. 4. All these children differ significantly in self-esteem as well as social esteem. 5. Crippled children were found to be facing various educational problems.

Bala (1985) worked on the comparative study of the mental make-ups and educational facilities for the physically handicapped and normal children. The major findings of the study were 1. Deaf, blind and orthopaedically handicapped children differed significantly from normal children in personality trait and values. 2. The adjustment of deaf children was less stable. 3. Blind children possessed poor, social, and perceived self-concept. 4. Orthopaedically handicapped children had a poor concept of their power and strength and had more negative tendencies.

Majority of studies conducted showed a positive and significant relationship between adjustment and academic achievement. This was true even when different tools were used to measure adjustment. In other words, those children who were well adjusted with their home, school, society, and their emotions achieved better academically and act a higher level than those who are ill adjusted in those areas of adjustments. Hence there is a need for the present study to consider adjustment as one of the variable, which would influence achievement of the crippled children very significantly. This has helped the researcher to construct the adjustment inventory.

Conclusion

This chapter helped, the researcher in the selection of tools for collection of data, analysis, defining the problem, formulation of hypotheses, formulation of objectives. It was possible to come up with specific recommendation by providing justification based on the present study and also keeping in view, the total perspective of studies in this area.

From what has been reviewed above, it may be concluded that;

1. Some of the findings of the studies discussed are contradictory in the light of these conflicting results it is of great importance to pursue the study and examine the problem in greater detail.
2. It may be further noted that studies reviewed above included only two or three variables as independent to find their relationships to academic achievement. No study has included four predictor variables of academic achievement.
3. Most of the studies have not investigated the factors affecting the academic achievement of physically handicapped pupils (Crippled).

4. Therefore, there is a need to bring together greater number of variables influencing academic achievement of physically handicapped pupils and to study their relative contribution in predicting academic achievement of physically handicapped pupils.

In this chapter, the researcher has discussed the importance of reviews and reviews related to self-concept and academic achievement, anxiety and academic achievement, achievement motivation and academic achievement, adjustment and academic achievement of physically handicapped children.

The next chapter deals with the discussion of variables selected, conceptual definitions of the terms used in the study, discussion of hypotheses, sampling procedure, a brief description and justification of tools used for data collection and analysis.

3

Methodology

INTRODUCTION

In the previous chapter, the review of the related literature concerning the self-concept, Anxiety, Achievement Motivation and Adjustment problems in relation to Academic Achievement was presented.

This chapter presents the methodology used by the researcher. It includes selection, and discussion of variables, definition of terms, formulation of hypotheses, tools used for collection of data, sampling technique, administration and scoring of the tests and Statistical techniques used for analysis of data.

A regular plan is a detailed description of a proposed study designed to investigate a given problem. It includes justification for the hypotheses to be tested; a detailed presentation of the research steps that will be followed in collecting and analyzing required data. A well thought out plan saves time, reduces probability of mistakes and generally results in higher quality of researches. (Gay, 1990,.)

Since, the researcher is involved in the study of self concept, Anxiety, Achievement Motivation and Adjustment problems in relation to Academic Achievement of the 9th standard physically handicapped children, the methodology developed by the researcher has been discussed in detail in the pages to follow.

STATEMENT OF THE PROBLEM

Study of adjustment problems of physically handicapped children of secondary schools in relation to their academic achievement, in Karnataka state, with reference to Chitradurga, Dharwad and Bellary districts.

SELECTIONS AND CLASSIFICATION OF VARIABLES

A variable is that factor which is measured, manipulated and observed by the investigator for the purpose of research.(Bruce Tuck man, 1978,.).

Independent Variable

An, Independent variable is a factor which is measured, manipulated, observed and selected by the investigator for the purpose of determining its relationship to an observed phenomenon. It is also called as input variable or the stimulus variable. (John Best, 1992,.).

The independent variable considered by the researcher in the present study is Self Concept, Anxiety, Achievement Motivation and Adjustment.

Dependent Variable

A dependent variable is one, which is measured, and observed by the investigator to determine the effect of independent variable on it. The dependent variable selected by the investigator in the present study is academic achievement of the handicapped children. The dependent variables are the measured changes in pupil performance to the influence of independent variables. (John Best, 1992,).

HYPOTHESES

A hypothesis is a tentative explanation for certain behavioral phenomenon or events that have occurred or (John Best, 1992). A hypothesis states the researcher's expectations concerning the relationship between the variables in the research problem. A hypothesis is the most specific statement of a problem .It states what the researcher thinks the outcome of the study will be (Gay, 1990).

Based upon the discussion of variables and also keeping the objectives in view the following hypotheses were formulated.

1. There is no significant difference in respect of the man scores of academic achievement of physically handicapped children belonging to high self-concept and low self-concept groups.
2. There is no significant difference in respect of the mean scores of academic achievement of physically handicapped children belonging to high anxiety and low anxiety groups.
3. There is no significant difference in the interaction between self-concept and anxiety on academic achievement.
4. There is no significant difference in respect of the mean scores of academic achievement of physically handicapped children belonging to high and low achievement motivation groups.
5. There is no significant difference in respect of the mean scores of academic achievement of physically handicapped children belonging to high and low self-concept groups.
6. There is no significant difference in the interaction between self-concept and achievement on academic achievement

   There is no significant difference in respect of the

mean scores of academic of physically handicapped children belonging to high and low adjustment groups.

7. There is no significant difference in respect of the mean scores of academic of physically handicapped children belonging to high and low self-concept groups.
8. There is no significant difference in the interaction between self-concept and adjustment on academic achievement.
9. There is no significant difference in respect of the mean scores of academic achievement of physically handicapped children belonging to high and low anxiety groups.
10. There is no significant difference in respect of the mean scores of academic achievement of physically handicapped children belonging to high and low achievement motivation groups.
11. There is no significant difference in the interaction between anxiety and achievement motivation on academic achievement.
12. There is no significant difference in respect of the mean scores of academic achievement of physically handicapped children belonging to high and low anxiety groups.
13. There is no significant difference in respect of the mean scores of academic achievement of physically handicapped children belonging to high and low adjustment groups.
14. There is no significant difference in the interaction between anxiety and adjustment on academic achievement.
15. There is no significant difference in respect of the

mean scores of academic achievement of physically handicapped children belonging to high and low achievement motivation groups.

16. There is no significant difference in the mean scores of academic achievement of physically handicapped children belonging to high and low adjustment groups.
17. There is no significant difference in the interaction between achievement groups.

DEFINITION OF THE TERMS

Self-Concept

In recent years the problem of self has come to the forefront in psychological thinking because of the realization of the need for an integrating concept to deal with the individuals experience and behavior. Without self the integrating factor in personality, behavioral episodes may appear to be diverse and unrelated. No part of the behaviors is free from self. Self is the nuclear concept of Roger's theory of personality (1961). It develops as a result of the interaction of the individual with this environment. The self strives for consistency. The individual acts largely in a way consistent with the self (Narayana Rao, 1989). It may be conceived as an organized Gestalt comprising:

1. The individual's perception of himself and the values attached to them.
2. The individual's perception of himself in relation to other persons and values attached to them.
3. Self-concept is influenced by the intensity with which one experiences the aspects of his environment.
4. Self-concept has direction.

The self-concept emphasizes the fact that in any judgments of personality the whole-person must always be considered. This means that conduct must serve as the basis of measurement and prediction.

The word "self concept" has been defined by different authors a few of them are discussed:

In the words of Bayed (1961) self concept is the fullest description of oneself of which a person is capable at any time, the self concept, therefore, is something that is developed through countless learning experience as the child integrates with others and with his environment, as he discovers himself. And as he becomes aware of what he is capable of doing and what cannot do.

According to Rogers (1969) "self concept" is the images of people have of themselves. They are composition of the beliefs they have about themselves, their physical, social, emotional characteristics, their achievements, it is the organized consistency conceptual Gestalt composed of perception of characterization of the "I" and "ME" and the relationships together with the values attached to these perceptions.

Ram Kumar (1973) defines the self-concept of an individual, as the congruency as expressed in the correlation between the self-concept as the individual perceives, and self-concept as we would like to possess.

Self-concept holds the key to self-confidence. The kinds of activities he engages, in his relationship with others and also in his achievement in general.

Self-concept has been referred by Lowe (1961) as one's attitude towards self and the same is referred to by Pederson (1965) as an organized configuration, or perception, belief, feelings, attitudes and values which the individual views as a part of characteristics of himself.

Anxiety

Anxiety is characterized by apprehension, uneasiness and foreboding from which the individual cannot escape, the anxious person feels blocked and unable to find a solution for his problem. Unlike fear, it does not come from a present situation. The anxious child is often unaware of the cause of its anxiety. The child seems to be unsuccessful in whatever he undertakes.

Anxiety, according to Jerslid (1960) is response to a hidden and subjective danger, while fear is a response to an objective danger.

Kolb (1968) describes anxiety, as a condition of heightened disruptive inner tension, accompanied by vague but often disquietly feeling of uneasiness and apprehension.

According to Bench (1968) Anxiety is a unpleasurable state of tension which indicates the presence of some danger to the organism or as the apprehensive tension of uneasiness which stems from the anticipation of danger in which the course is largely unknown or unrecognized.

Chaplin (1968) defines anxiety as a feeling of singled dread and apprehension about the future without specific cause for the fear.

Mussen (1970) defines anxiety, as referring to an affective state of the individual, characterized by fearfulness, or dread.

Horney (1970) says that, anything that disturbs the security of the child in relation to his parents (such as rejection, over protection, harsh punishment, inconsistent treatment etc.) May produce basic anxiety. He defines basic anxiety as "the feeling a child has of being isolated and helpless in a potentially hostile world"(1945). Insecure child is an effort to cope with his basic anxiety. He may become hostile and aggressive and develop a neurotic need for power over other. He may strive excessively for the affection. Approval or admiration of those he may develop a neurotic ambition for personal achievement or constantly strive for perfection or he may withdraw from relationship with others self efficiently and independence.

In the words of Sinha (1966) Anxiety is the response of an individual to a hidden danger, a fear of possible failure or punishment in future. Anxiety has been observed to manifest itself in different spheres of life.

This scale includes the anxiety reactions to the following areas.

- Health, Appearance and Injury
- Areas of Ambition
- Family Anxieties
- Anxieties regarding Friendship and love
- Physiological and psychological manifestation

Achievement Motivation

Achievement motivation is not a new concept in the word of motivation. It is essentially a type of motivation is personal in nature.

The basis of achievement motivation is a motive to achieve. Those who engage themselves in a task on account of an achievement motive are said to work under the spirit of achievement motivation. If a child decides to improve the performance at school or to get a good grade it is known as achievement motivation.

Atkinson and Feather (1975) says, "The Achievement motive is conceived as a latent disposition which is manifested in overt disposition which is manifested in overt striving only when the individual perceives performance as instrumental to a sense of personal accomplishment.

In the words of McClelland and Atkinson (1975) "Achievement motivation may be associated with variety of goals, but in general the behavior adopted will involve activity which is directed towards the attainment of some standard of excellence." From the view of Deo Mohan (1920), Achievement motivation is a devise which can be aroused by inducing a situation of ego involvement of achievement orientation. It is characterized by a desire to attain a high standard of excellence and to accomplish the unique objectives.

Adjustment

Adjustment is a process of continuous interaction between the organism and its environment. A child from the moment of birth is continually being acted upon by various social agencies like the family, school, religious institution, peergroup. Various cultural organizations, clubs etc. These agencies along with the social setting in which the child is born, and the way in which the child takes and reacts in these situations, are the determining factors in the development of personality of the child. Adjustment has been variously defined by the various psychologists.

Thorndike and Hagen (1960) defines adjustment as: adjustment will mean the behavior pattern that enables a person to get along with and be comfortable in his social setting.

Alexander (1960) defines adjustment as a "process involving better mental and behavioral responses by which an individual strives to cope successfully with inner needs, tensions, frustrations, and conflicts and to effect a degree of harmony between the inner demands and those imposed on him by the objectives world in which he lives." Allport (1962) says that "personality is the dynamic organization of the psycho-physical system, that determines his unique adjustment to his environment."

Cattle (1964) says that when an internal and external adjustment is made by the organism, the individual with such an adjustment can devote most of his energy to the attainment of satisfactory purpose and goals.

Concentration, learning, reasoning and other mental activities are adversely affected by personality maladjustment. As a result of this, individual will perform below their intellect capacities. Conversely personality adjustment may result in higher level of academic achievement.

In other words, a well-adjusted pupil is capable of facing hard realities of life. They are bold enough to meet any sort of obstacle, which comes in their way of academic persuits cordially and unemotionally. A good adjustment result in the higher level of academic achievement. In the present study the following areas are considered in the adjustment, health adjustment, home adjustment and educational adjustment. These terms are discussed in the succeeding paragraphs.

(a) *Social Adjustment:* refers to the capacity of the individual to react adequately to social relation, situations and relations with others.

(b) *Emotional Adjustment:* Refers to the emotional aspect of the individual in which he is able to control his behavior in terms of his emotions where as the tensions is almost minimized.

(c) *Home Adjustment:* Refers to the individual helping himself to the expectation of his parents in carrying out his duties assigned to him and feels satisfied about his role, and position in the home and his ability to have a easeful relationships.

(d) *Health Adjustment:* Health in the human organism is that condition that permits optimal functioning of the individuals, enabling him to live and to serve best in personal and social relationships.

(e) *Educational Adjustment:* In the education of children with motor handicaps, premium is placed on intellectual development, academic ability, and facilitating the child's total adjustment to limitations. In schools, he can be aided in living better as a child and prepared to face the future. Acquisition of skills will be of considerable importance to the child. Through these skills he can increase his understanding of the world in which he lives, and he can communicate more effectively.

Academic Achievement

Academic achievement as such generally refers to the grade obtained in the annual examination. Academic achievement is seen by Mellinger and Haggard as "an expression of one way the individual learns to utilize his energies, given certain innate potentials pattern of socializing pressure".

Academic achievement is influenced by various factors and in turn academic achievement influence as individual's level of aspiration in social and occupational status. To define academic success one has to look at it from different perspective.

From a sociological point of view, the most important determinant of a person's adult status in western societies as Britain and U.S.A. was generally his occupation. Thus academic success is judged in terms of social status.

From a psychological point of view academic success might be defined in terms of the acquisition of different kinds of knowledge and cognitive skills. In some respect the multidimensional description which one could then have would be theoretically most satisfactory. It would however, make comparison among people extremely different" and in practices, the evidence usually available is only of attainments in one or two aspects of school work of average attainment with the particular skills assessed and generally being specified. Such crude measures of attainment are closely related to the formal academic qualification.

Academic achievement of an individual attainment in scholastic subject prescribed for a particular course of study. In this study academic achievement would mean the total attainment of the student as measured by the marks obtained by them in the core subjects prescribed by the Government of Karnataka.

TOOLS USED FOR THE COLLECTION

To carry out any type of research on, a researcher will require many data gathering tools or techniques which help him to test the hypothesis. The word tool in evaluation is defined as an implement or a means to collect evidence. In research it is necessary to acquire sufficient reliable data of many kind and employ distinctive ways of describing and quantifying the data. Each tool is particularly appropriate for certain source of data, yielding information of the kind and in the form that could be most effectively used John Best, 1992).

For the present study the following tools were used for collecting the required data, as they were found to be appropriate.

1. Vansant Ram Kumar Q-sort set for measuring self-concept. (Appendix A)
2. Sinha's Manifest Anxiety scale for measuring Anxiety. (Appendix B)
3. Deo-Mohan' achievement motivation scale for measuring achievement. (Appendix C)
4. Adjustment inventory developed by the researcher. (Appendix G)

5. Achievement test constructed by the researcher of the students. (Appendix E)

DESCRIPTION OF THE TOOLS

Self-Concept

To measure self concept, adopted version of Vasantha Kumar was used. It is an appropriate tool used for measuring self concept especially when it is defined as the congruences between perceived self concept and ideal self concept.

This scale was used by the researcher like Nagaraju (1977) and Kongawad (1998). It is easy for the students to sort out the words. It was translated to Kannada by Shivappa (1985) the scale consist of forty-one descriptive words. It is easy for the students to sort out the words the students were required to sort them twice online point scale, the first sorting was based on the students ideal self. The first four points were positive in description and the fifth was a neutral point and remaining four points on the scale were negative in description. Each point on the scale had to be filled with a specific number of words, which has to be selected from the forty-one words given.

Again the same words were given and students were required to sort out again in the same manner as they did earlier and the criterion of selections of words was based on their perceived self, in other words, students sorted out the words based on their feelings.

Administration and Scoring

1. The scale was administrated to the 9th standard crippled students studying in handicapped schools, during the morning session.

2. The resulting two sets of scores sorting on nine-point scale were correlated to get the extent of congruence between

the ideal selves and perceived self. This value of correlations denoted the self-concept.

Scoring Key

The marks allotted for the first four positive terms 5th is neutral and further last fur negative terms is as follows.

4	3	2	1	0	-1	-2	-3	-4

Validity

Expert's opinions were obtained to establish the validity of the inventory 100 items was given to 5 psychologists to classify the items to the category to which it belongs. Items of highest agreement, which are not less than 80% of agreement, were selected. Thus the content validity was established.

The correlation was established between self-concept and achievement scores. It was found to be 0.25, which shows a significant positive correlation.

The predictive validity was established by correlation the self-concept scores with achievement. It was found by Nagaraju, (1977). That the predictive validity was moderately high. (r=0.57, n=90). The reliability was established with a sample of 78 students by using test retest method. The gap was 3 weeks in between the administration. The co-relation obtained between 2 successive administrations was 0.63. This was found to be fairly high. Appendix.

Sinha's Manifest Anxiety Scale

Sinha's Manifest Anxiety Scale: Durgananda Sinha's Anxiety scale (1966) was used in the present study to obtain the measure of the manifest anxiety of the crippled children. The scale consists of 100 statements. These statements are designed to elicit self rating on items describing the anxiety reactions to the areas such as health, family, friendship, and love, social reactions, civilization, virtue, future, guilt, and shame, physical and physiological manifestations, etc. The students were asked to check each statement as true or false as applied to the individual taking the test. The maximum score that any one could get was 100; True statement carries "one" mark. False statement carries "Zero" mark.

Administration and Scoring

This scale was administered to 9th standard crippled students studying in handicapped school. The Sinha anxiety scale is easy to administer and fulfills all the required objectives. It is for the students to respond. It was translated to Kannada by Shivappa (1985). The researcher strictly followed the instructions prescribed by the author while administering the scale.

Scoring

The scale can be scored accurately by hand, and no scoring key or stencil was provided, for any response indicated as "yes", the testee snould be awarded the score of "one", and "zero" for no. The sum of all the positive or "yes" responses would be the total anxiety scale of the individual.

For reliability and validity of the scale the test-retest reliability index was computed on a try out sample of 85 students with a gap of five weeks and it was found to be 0.85, whereas by split-half method on a try-out sample of 239 students it was found to be 0.92.

The score on Taylor's manifest anxiety scale was used as the first validation criterion. The correlation against Taylor's MAS was fond to be 0.69; against Dutt's anxiety questionnaire, it was found to be 0.72; and against Cattells I PAT anxiety scale questionnaire, it was found to be 0.70 (Appendix B).

Deo-Mohan's Achievement Motivation Scale

To measure the achievement motivation of crippled

children Deo-Mohan's Achievement Motivation Scale was used. Which was translated to Kannada by Kangawad (1992) it is easy to administer, items in the scale were based on 1. academic, 2. Factors of general interest, and 3. factors of social interest.

The scale consists of 50 items (13 negative and 37 positive items) relating to fifteen factors. The items were distributed as; 4 items on academic motivation; 4 items on need for challenge achievement: 4 items on academic challenge: 1items on achievement anxiety; 2 items on importance of grades/ marks; 4 items on meaning fullness of taks; 2 items on relevance of school to future goals; 4 items on attitude towards education; 5 items on work methods; 3 items on attitude towards teachers; 4 items on interpersonal relation; 2 items on dramatics; and 5 items on sports. The students is required to respond to each items on the 5 items scale-always, frequently, sometimes, rarely and never in such a way or to describe the way in which he is generally motivated. The positive items are scored as 4, 3, 2, 1, or 0 and negative items as 0, 1, 2, 3, 4, 5, depending upon the responses of the students to items; sum total of all the scores varies from 0 to 200 and represents the individual's achievement motivations.

Administration and Scoring

This scale was administered to 9th standard crippled students studying in physically handicapped schools.

The researcher strictly followed the instruction prescribed by the author while administering the scale. Assurance was given to the students that the response obtained will be kept confidential and used for the research purposes only.

Along with above instruction the researcher read the instruction given in the scale. There are 50 items in it (out of 50 items, 13items are negative and 37 items are positive.) Against each item there are five responses. Obtained will be kept confidential and used for the research purpose only.

Along with above instructions the research read the instructions given in the scale. There are 50 items in it (out of 50 items, 13 items are negative and 37 items are positive). Against each items there are five responses. They have to read each item carefully and respond top it by marking on any one of the five responses given against that items.

There was no right or wrong answer. The right answers was only what they feel about themselves with reference to that statement. The researcher informed that their answers will be kept confidential.

Scoring

The respondent is provided with five alternatives to give his responses ranging from always to not at all. The3 alternative or responses are arranged in such a way that the scoring system for all the positive items will remain as 4, 3, 2, 1,and 0 and scoring system for negative items will as 0, 1, 2, 3, 4 and 4. If the respondent put (x) mark for first alternative the score is 4 for second alternative the score is 3 for third alternative the score is 2 for the fourth it is 1 and for the fifth and last alternative the score is 'zero'.

In a similar way for negative item if the respondent put (x) mark for the first alternative. The score is 0 for the second alternative the score is 1, for the third alternative the score is 2, for the fourth the second alternative the score is 3 and for the fifth alternative the score is 4.The summated scores of all the 50 items provides total achievement motivation scores of an individual responses are obtained on the test booklet itself. The reliability co-efficient of the scale by the test retest method with an interval of 4 weeks for mixed groups is 0.69(n =51); 5-6 weeks for boys is 0.67; 5-6 weeks for girls is 0.78 which were significant at 0.01 level.

As far as the validity is concerned, the co-efficient of correlation between the scale and projective test was 0.54

was found to be 0.75(n =93); against McCleveland's projective measures. These co-efficient of reliability and validity were sufficiently high and the scale was considered as valid and reliable (Appendix C).

Achievement Test

It is designed to measure the objective such as knowledge, application and skills in a specified subject or group of subject. The achievement tests are concerned with the quantity and quality of learning attained in a subject of study, or group of subject after a period of instruction educational achievement tests involve some of the psychological processes measured with tests if intelligence, they utilize specific materials from an area of subject matter in which instruction has been provided. Their purpose is to measure how much has been learned in the subject and what specific abilities or skills have been developed. An achievement test is essentially a tool for device for measurement that help in ascertaining quantity of learning attained in a subject of study or groups of subject after a period of instruction. It also measures the present ability of the individual concerned. (Mangal, 1985).

The researcher constructed an achievement test in the core Subject for the 9th standard Kannada medium childrens. As there are no scientifically developed achievement test available to the researcher for the present syllabus to measure the achievement of the 9th standard children. The core subjects included in the test were General Science, General Mathematics and Social Studies as prescribed by the government of Karnataka.

Purpose of the Test

To know the academic achievement of 9th standard crippled children studying in physically handicapped school.

Construction of the Achievement Test

An Achievement test was constructed keeping in mind

the objectives such as knowledge, comprehension, application and skills of the students. The textbook prescribed by the Government of Karnataka for IX standard was used is the construction of the test.

A blueprint of the achievement test in general mathematics, general science and social science was prepared by the researcher (given in the appendix J.K.L) and suggestion regarding weight ages o be assigned to the contents and objectives were decided in consultation with the experts, the senior teachers and teachers-educators, in general science, general mathematics and social science.

In consonance with the above objectives the test items were prepared. The items were of the multiple-choice type with four choices each. Standardized tests usually contain multiple choice type items. Ebel (1965) while discussing the merits of the multiple choices says. "Almost any understanding or ability that can be tested by means of any other item form short answer, completion, true-false, matching or essay type can also be tested by means of multiple choice test items. Since the responses to the items had to be subjected to item analysis. Which result in the discarding of few items that fail to measure up to the required standard, a little mor than the required number was prepared. The items prepared by the researcher were ṣubjected to security by a experts. Their suggestions were incorporated in respect to certain items and thus the items were refined 70 items were prepared in each subject for IX standard i.e., in General Science, 70 items, in general mathematics 70 items, and social science 70 items.

After the construction of the test, it is ready to be given a trial in actual use, "since it is impossible to know in advance how good the test is, or to eliminate all the poor items, a tryout is essential (Stanley Julliom 1964). It was administered to a sample of 185 students drawn from the following schools for the tryout as shown in the table below.

TABLE IV

Name of the Scools and Number

Number of schools and number of students for pilot study

Siddalingeshwara Residential Integrated Handicapped Schools.

1.	Kannamadagu (Bellary).	25
2.	S.J.M. Handicapped Residential high school, Haveri (Dharwad)	60
3.	Sri Ranganathaswamy Residential High School, Malebennur (Chitradurga)	60
4.	Vishwakalyana Mahila Vidya Samithi Residential Integrated High School, Hubli (Dt. Dharwad)	40
	Total	185

The time for the test was not restricted. However, the students were informed to complete as early as they can. All the three tests were administered on the same day simultaneously with the help of the assistant teachers in all the schools after allowing a gap of 45 minutes between each test.

Purpose of Try Out

As per Ebel (1965) the purposes of try out are

1. To identify weak or defective items to reveal the necessary improvement. To identify ambiguous, indeterminate, implausible distracters very difficult and very easy items.
2. To determine the difficulty value of each items. It facilitates selection and placement of items for final form.
3. To determine the discrimination value of each item.
4. To determine the number of items to be included in the final test.
5. To fix the time limit.

Scoring

The answers were hand scored according to the predetermined key. Each correct answer was assigned one mark. The total number of corrected answers yielded the individual total scores.

Item Analysis

Both the reliability and the validity of a test depend ultimately upon the characteristics of the items, which make up the test. It follows that any test can be improved through selection, substitution or revision of items.

According to Ebel (1965), "The analysis of student response to objective test items is a powerful tool for test improvement. Item analysis indicates which item may be too easy or too difficult and which may fall or other reasons to discriminate clearly between the better and the poorer examinee".

The item analysis of the test gives us two kinds of information. It gives us the idea about the difficulty index of the items and the index of discrimination. Thus the item analysis is a statistical device to reveal the quality of each test item.

Index of Item Difficulty

Noll (1965) item difficulty is concerned with finding how difficult an item and is determined by the percentage of pupils passing it. Items which are answered correctly or which are missed by all the pupils are not considered as good, for such items make discrimination. A test made up of only such items would result in everyone getting the same score. Obviously, such a result tells nothing about differences in achievement among members of the class. Rather it demonstrates that the test was either too easy or too difficult. The value of index of difficulty ranges from 0 to 100. Higher the index easier will be the item. The difficulty index is calculated by using the formula.

$$D= \frac{N_H+N_L}{N_T} \times 100$$

Where D- Difficulty index.

N- number in high group answering the item correctly.

N- number is low group answering the item correctly.

N -total number of pupils who answered that item.

Index of Discrimination

The discrimination power of individual items tells on the quality of the item to differentiate superior and inferior students. It has been regarded as an indicator of validity.

The index of discrimination is determined by using the formula.

$$d = \frac{N_n - N_l}{N}$$

Where d= discrimination index.

N- number in high group answering the i N- number in low group answering the item correctly.~

N –Total number either in high or low group.

The index of discrimination is the main criterion in final form.

Ebel 91965) has suggested a criterion to select items based on index of discrimination. The criterion is as in Table V.

Process of Item Analysis

Ebel (1965) considers item analysis a process of dividing the test scores into two groups and then comparing the individual item responses of each group. The following steps as suggested by Ebel were followed in this study.

TABLE V

Criteria for Selection of Items Based on Index of Discrimination

Index of discrimination	*Item evaluation*
0.40 and above	Very good items.
0.3 to 0.39	Reasonably good items but Possibly subject to improvement
0.20 to 29	Marginal items usually Needing and being
Below 0.19	poor items to be rejected or improved.

They were:

1. The scored answer sheets were arranged in the order of scores, from high to low.
2. Two subgroups of test papers ere repeated out, an upper group consisting of approximately 27% of the total group who received the highest score on the test, and a lower group consisting of an equal number of papers from those who received the lower scores.
3. A time analysis chart was prepared. This contains the record of responses counts of both the groups to each item with the correct answer indicated.
4. The index of difficulty was computed.
5. The index of discrimination was worked out.

Item index revealed that only 50 items were retained out of 70 items. The item difficulty and discrimination level of the achievement test is given; in table VI

TABLE VI

Difficulty Level and Index of Discrimination of the Items Selected for Achievement Battery for Standard

Science (Physics)

Sl. No.	*Item No.*	*Difficulty Index*	*Discrimination Index*
1.	2	67	0.54
2.	4	56	0.56
3.	5	52	0.44
4.	6	54	0.52
5.	8	74	0.52
6.	9	74	0.52
7.	10	76	0.4
8.	11	64	0.65
9.	12	50	0.44
10.	14	61	0.78
11.	15	60	0.64
12	16	68	0.6
13.	18	65	0.48
14.	19	57	0.5
15.	21	65	0.48
16.	23	55	0.58

Science (Chemistry)

Sl.No.	*Item No.*	*Difficulty Index*	*Discrimination Index*
1.	24	77	0.42
2.	26	79	0.4
3.	29	58	0.6
4.	30	70	0.56
5.	32	80	0.4
6.	33	77	0.4
7.	35	56	0.72

contd...

Sl.No.	*Item No.*	*Difficulty Index*	*Discrimination Index*
8.	37	74	0.52
9.	39	77	0.42
10.	40	30	0.48
11.	41	37	0.5
12.	43	72	0.42
13.	45	61	0.58
14.	46	74	0.4
15.	47	75	0.58
16.	48	72	0.52
17.	49	72	0.4
18.	51	72	0.52

Sl. No.	*Item No*	*Difficulty Indux*	*Discrimination Index*
1.	2	67	0.54

Science (Biology)

Sl.No.	*Item No.*	*Difficulty Index*	*Discrimination Index*
1.	53	63	0.52
2.	54	75	0.12
3.	55	57	0.82
4.	57	69	0.58
5.	59	69	0.58
6.	60	67	0.62
7.	61	47	0.42
8.	62	62	0.56
9.	64	47	0.42
10.	65	37	0.42
11.	67	70	0.56
12.	68	65	0.5
13.	69	72	0.4
14.	70	45	0.54
15.	72	70	0.56
16.	73	67	0.46

TABLE VI

Showing the Selected Items Based on the Difficulty Index & Discrimination Index

Maths , Social Studies

Sl. No.	*Item*	*Diffi.*	*Discri. Index index*	*Item no. index*	*Diffi-index*
1.	2	65	0.5	2	77
2.	4	70	0.44	3	76
3.	6	66	0.52	5	71
4.	9	37	0.42	6	60
5.	10	36	0.48	8	38
6.	12	37	0.66	9	69
7.	14	66	0.52	10	43
8.	15	45	0.46	11	50
9.	17	38	0.8	12	68
10.	18	48	0.76	13	37
11.	19	57	0.5	14	77
12.	20	57	0.66	16	54
13.	22	48	0.44	17	76
14.	23	67	0.46	18	40
15.	24	60	0.64	20	51
16.	25	64	0.48	21	76
17.	26	68	0.48	22	71
18.	27	62	0.48	24	62
19.	30	45	0.54	25	60
20.	32	60	0.56	26	41
21.	33	62	0.56	27	55
22.	34	56	0.76	28	72
23.	37	55	0.5	29	75
24.	38	57	0.5	30	68
25.	39	35	0.42	31	61
26.	41	62	0.56	32	6

contd...

Sl. No.	*Item*	*Diffi.*	*Discri. Index index*	*Item no. index*	*Diffi-index*
27.	42	57	0.58	33	70
28.	43	62	0.64	35	36
29.	44	65	0.46	37	69
30.	45	72	0.4	38	51
31.	46	47	0.42	39	60
32.	47	61	0.5	41	43
33.	48	70	0.52	42	78
34.	49	63	0.52	43	34
35.	50	69	0.58	45	69
36.	52	70	0.56	46	43
37.	53	80	0.4	47	71
38.	55	56	0.72	48	76
39.	56	77	0.42	49	77
40.	57	30	0.48	52	43
41.	58	37	0.5	53	50
42.	60	69	0.44	55	68
43.	62	67	0.62	57	65
44.	63	45	0.5	60	61
45.	65	62	0.56	61	61
46.	66	70	0.44	62	5
47.	58	77	0.42	64	75
48.	69	56	0.7	65	68
49.	71	57	0.5	67	74
50.	72	38	0.8	70	67

Final Test

The final test was administered to a sample of 100 children studying in the IX standard. The researcher administered the test in all schools at the same day simultaneously with the help of the co-operative teachers.

Directions were given to the pupils and they were asked to encircle for the number given for the correct answer from among the four choices, provided for each item. The number of items in each subject and the time limit are given in table below.

TABLE VII

Sl. No.	*Subject*	*No. of items*	*Time Limit*	*Marks*
1.	Gen. Math's	50	59 min	50
2.	Gen. Science	50	55 min	50
3.	Social Studies	50	48 min	50

During the try out of the test, the researcher had noted down the time of first five students and last five students who completed the test. From this the testing time for general mathematics, general sciences and social studies was determined. They were found to be 59 min. 55 min. and 48 mi. respectively.

Reliability and Validity of the Achievement Test

The term reliability has been considered by Anne (1982) as the consistency of the scores obtained by the same individual on different occasions or with different sets of equivalent forms. For the present study the test retest method was used to find out the reliability coefficient. In this method the same test is given twice to the same group and the score pairs correlated to obtain what is called reliability coefficient. The reliability co-efficient obtained for the IX standard whole test was 0.97, which indicates that the test was highly reliable. And for each subject reliability was found to be 0.66 for gen. Math's, 0.78 for Gen Science and 0.55 for Social studies. All these were found to be highly reliable.

Validity of the Test

The validity of a test or measuring instrument depends upon the fidelity with which it measures what it purposes to measure, (Garrett, 1979).

For the present study only the content validity was applied for validity of the test. Content validity involves the systematic examination of the content to determine whether it covers major objectives, such as application of principles, the factual knowledge. The researcher prepared a blue print for the achievement test and along with blue print, question paper was also given to the subject expert and teachers for scrutiny.

This was how the content validity was found out (For final achievement test appendix D, E, F, and for achievement test key answer appendix H.

Construction of an Adjustment Inventory

The review of literature revealed the non-availability of a tool to measure the adjustment problems of the physically handicapped children. The researcher therefore, collected the material relating to the development of the inventory for adjustment from various sources, (Freemen 1962). The researcher has collected problems relating to the adjustment directly from the students through interview and also researcher has asked the students to give their opinion through writing the problems facing by themselves the researcher has also collected the suggestions from the teachers and heads of the institution from the handicapped schools, and also the researcher has discussed the problems of the children with their parents.

Further, various techniques developed to measure adjustment revealed that these measures have not incorporated many important components of the adjustment presumed in theory and in observation, these measures do not deal with all aspects of adjustment of children of the age group 13. Hence the researcher selected a few components of the adjustments inventory and given them to a panel of experts (a few psychologists and hostel superintendent of the handicapped students. for scrutiny. The components were finalized by incorporating the suggestions given by the experts. The following areas were included in the adjustment inventory, social, emotional, home, health and education.

The word adjustment will mean the behavior patterns that enable a person to get along with and be comfortable in his social setting. (Thorndike and Hagen).

Collecting and Editing of Statements

After finalizing the areas of the adjustment inventory the next step was to write statements on those areas based on the collected material from various sources like students, teachers and parents.

The researcher initially selected a total of 100 statements from the five areas such as social, emotional, home, health and education. Care was taken to see that statements suited to the maturity level of the students of 9th standard. Each statement was provided with the choices true or false. The student is required to read each statement and encircle 'T' if he feels the statement is true or encircle 'F' if it's false.

Scoring and Editing of Statements: Pre Try Out of Adjustment Inventory

These 100 statements were given to a panel of experts for scrutiny. After the scrutiny by the experts 85 statements were selected by incorporating the suggestions given by them the remaining 15 statements were discarded for technical difficulties. The 85 statements were then developed into an inventory with an appropriate format. (APPENDIX 'G').

Try-Out Procedure

The researcher tried out the adjustment inventory on a sample of 50 students from two schools one situated at Malebennur and another at Holalkere. The clear directions were given to the students about how to record their responses. The details are found in table VIII about the number of samples selected from the different schools. The samples included both boys and girls. The number of statements included under different areas of adjustment inventory for the purpose of try out procedure is given in the table IX

Purposes of Try-Out

Lindquist (1961) lists various purposes served by a try-out they are:

1. To identify weaker defective statements and to reveal needed improvements.
2. To provide data needed to determine how many statements should constitute the inventory.
3. To provide data needed to determine appropriate time limits for the inventory.
4. To discover weaknesses or needed improvements in the mechanics of inventory taking in the directions to the examiner and so forth.

TABLE VIII

Number of Students and Schools Selected for the Try-Out of Adjustment Inventory

Sl. No	*School*	*No. of students*
1.	Sree Ranganathaswamy Residential Handicapped integrated education high schoolMalebennur, District. Chitradurga.	35
2.	Sree Ekanatheswara residential handicapped integrated education high school, Holalkere, district. Chitradurga.	15
	Total	50

TABLE IX

Areas and the Number of Statements included in Adjustment Inventory for Try-Out

Sl. No.	*Areas of adj. inventory*	*No. ofstatement*
1.	Social adjustment	15
2.	Emotional adjustment	24
3.	Home adjustment	15
4.	Health adjustment	13
5.	Educational adjustment	18
	Total	85

Scoring of the Adjustment Inventory

The respondent is provided with two answers to give response either true or false. Depending on the nature of the statement, each may have a score of 1 or zero. Zero is given where researcher finds adjustment and a score of one is given where there is no adjustment. Area wise scores are written and the total score is found which indicates the lack of adjustment.

Selection of Statement for Final Adjustment on the Basis of Chi-Square Value

The value of chi-square is a measure of the extent to which a given statement differentiates between the well and low adjusted groups. It may be regarded that any chi-square value equal or greater than 3.84 as indicating the average response of the well and low groups to a statement differing significantly provided. It contains 25 well-adjusted and 25 poorly adjusted students.

The researcher determined the chi-square value for all 85 statements of the adjustment inventory .The size of chi-square value ranged from 3.84 to 20.16 the statement having chi-square value less than 3.84 was selected form the inventory. Thus, finally 75 statements whose chi-square value was more than 3.84 were selected for the final administration of the adjustment inventory. The statement selected together with their chi-square value were found in the below table X.

TABLE X(Appen)

Number of Statements Selected for Adjustment Inventory with Their Chi-Square Value

The statements were then grouped under each dimension of the adjustment inventory based on the magnitude of their chi-square value. These 75 statements were then rearranged randomly by taking lots and then were developed into the final form of the adjustment inventory appendix with appropriate directions for the students to record their responses. The number of statement selected for final administration of the adjustment inventory on different areas is given in the Table XI.

TABLE XI

Areas and the Number of Statements Included in the Adjustment Inventory for Final Administration

Sl. No.	*Areas of adjustment inventory*	*Items*
1.	Social	13
2.	Emotional	22
3.	Home	13
4.	Health	10
5.	Educational	17
	Total	75

Areas and the number of statements included in the adjustment inventory for final administration.

Final Administration and Scoring of the Adjustment Inventory

After finalizations of the sampling procedures, the next

step was to carry out the final administration of the adjustment. The inventory was administered to a sample of 100 students of 9th standard from the three district details are found in table XII. The students were made to be seated comfortably while taking the test. Besides this the following points were kept in view during the entire process of test administration.

1. The inventory was administered when the examiner were fresh and had adequate readiness.
2. Directions were given exactly as provided in the cover page of the inventory.
3. Before answering, the pupils were instructed to fill in the necessary information as asked on the title page of inventory.
4. Examples were thoroughly explained.

Administration of the Adjustment Inventory and Scoring

In the addition to the above instruction the researcher has given the following instructions to the students:

1. As it is self-administering inventory. The examiner should read the instruction given on the front page and examinees should also read them silently along with the examiner.

1. There is no time limit for answering it ordinarily an individual takes 10 minutes in completing the test.
2. Examiner should be instructed to interpret the meaning of sentences themselves. However the examiner should give meaning of the difficult words, if any.
3. Cooperation of the examiner in answering the inventory is very essential. The examiner should assure them that their answers and scores will be treated with confidence.

4. The examiners should indicate frankly and honestly the purpose of test, if and when any question regarding this is raised by the examiners.
5. They have to encircle for the term "yes" or "no" given against the each statement.

Scoring

Inventory can be scored by hand only for any answer indicative of adjustment zero is given. Otherwise score of one is awarded. Appendix-I shows the key response indicative of lack of adjustment. The total scores indicates the general adjustment status.

TABLE XII

Name of the District, School and Number of Students Selected for the Final Administration

Sl. No.	*District*	*Name of the School*	*No. of Students*
1.	Chitradurga district	Sri Mailara Lingeshwara Physically handicapped Residential integrated Education High school.	30
2.	Dharwad district	Sree Sarwajnamurthy Physically Handicapped Residential integrated Education High school	40
3.	Bellary district	Sree veerabhadreshwara Physically handicapped Residential Integrated Education High School	30
	Total		100

Determination of the reliability and validity of the adjustment inventory.

Any tool of research must contain the characteristics of a good measuring instrument. Among them validity and reliability are considered to be the most important characteristics of any good measuring instruments. Therefore, the researcher established the reliability of the adjustment inventory, which was developed by her. For this purpose the researcher followed the test-retest technique.

In this method the same test is read ministered shortly after the first administration and the two sets of scores are correlated to obtain the reliability of the test. The immediate memory effects practice and the confidence induced by familiarity in the test material may over estimate the reliability of the test, on the other hand, if the time interval is long, the real changes in behaviour in terms of growth may underestimate the reliability of the test. The reliability co-efficient obtained for the sample of 9th standard students (r= 0.92). Which indicates that the test developed was highly reliable.

To determine the validity, the researcher validated the adjustment inventory against Bell's adjustment inventory.

For the purpose, the researcher administered both the tools to a sample of IX standard, the coefficient of correlation was computed and found to be 0.98.

These co-efficient clearly demonstrate that the adjustment inventory is both valid and reliable.

Sampling

The primary purpose of a research is to discover principles that have universal application. But to study a whole population in order to arrive at a generalization would be impracticable. Sometimes the characteristics of the population cannot be measured, before the measurement could be completed, the population would have changed. (John Best, 1982).

For this purpose, the sampling makes it possible to draw valid inference or generalizations on the basis of careful observation of variables within a relatively small portion of the population.

The study is confined to the children IX standard studying in schools for physically handicapped located in Karnataka state during the year 1996- 97. There were 27 schools for physically handicapped in the state during the year 1996-97.

The sample considered for the present study included IX standard (Kannada medium) children studying in schools for physically handicapped located in Chitradurga, Dharwad and Bellary districts, location of these schools along with the number of children studying in Ix standard was given in the table XII.

These districts were selected because; they are near the place of the researcher. In all these districts these schools are specially run for the benefit of crippled children. These districts have only one special education school.

From the population of 27 schools for physically handicapped 3 schools with 100 children at IX standard were selected at random. From the three districts for selecting the children from each school of physically handicapped random sampling technique was used.

STATISTICAL TECHNIQUE ANALYSIS OF VARIANCE(ANOVA)

The analysis of variance (F) t-test is an inferential procedure, which have been treated exclusively in the context of testing hypothesis. The results of these tests provide techniques for treating the questions of, whether the observed phenomenon is likely to be attributable to chance or whether there is considerable probability that non-chance factors are in operations. In other words, they determined whether the results of statistical tests are 'significant' or not.

The 'F' and ' t test of significance are used whenever the distribution is normal and also when the sample is selected on random basis. In the present study the researcher has used both F and t test of significance to test the hypotheses because the nature of the sample fulfils the above two conditions,

Analysis of variance provides the researcher with a technique for simultaneously testing whether means of two or more groups are significantly different. It capitalizes on the integral relationship between the mean and the variance so that, by analyzing the variances of several groups, conclusions can be drawn regarding the similarity of the means of these groups.

It is a powerful statistical test, which can be used for a number of more complex models; the basis form of the technique is single classification of analysis of variance. In which the researcher has to organize his data in such a fashion that he is testing for differences in a dependent variable among groups which represent the consequences of a single independent variable.

A more complex form of this model is known as multiple classification analyses of variance, the relationship between one dependent variable and two or more independent variable can be tested. It is represented as F

$$F = \frac{\text{Between Group Variation}}{\text{Within Group variation}}$$

Any educational experiment involving more than one independent variable and each variable at different levels is known as factorial design. This is a widely used design in experimental and quasi-experimental research design. (Malcolm, Lindquest).

Data was analyzed by using multiple classification of Analysis of variances; this was preferred because the variables under consideration were divided into 2x2 design where each factor varied at 2 levels.

In this chapter, the researcher discussed the methodology followed by her. It includes selecting and discussion of variables, formulation of hypotheses, sampling procedure, tools used for collection of data and analysis of the data.

4

Analysis and Interpretation of Data

INTRODUCTION

In the previous chapter, the researcher presented a detailed account of the methodology used in the present study.

This included the discussion of variables, formulaion of hypothesis, selection of tools for collection, and analysis of data, details regarding the construction of adjustment inventory and achievement test in the core subject for 9th standard students: establishing the reliability and validity of the tools constructed by the researcher in order to obtain the required samples.

Execution of research study usually produce a mass of raw data resulting from the administration of standardized of self developed instruments, collected data must be accurately scored systematically organized in a manner that facilities analysis Gay (1990). Analysis means categorizing, ordering manipulating and summarizing of the data to obtain answer to research question .The purpose of analysis is to reduce data to intelligible and interpretable form so that the relation of research problem can be studied and tested. Interpretation takes the result of analysis, makes interferences pertinent to the research relations studied and draw conclusions about these relation. The researcher who interprets results reaches them for their meaning and implication. Kerlinger (1983).

The present chapter is devoted to the analysis and interpretation of data 2 X 2 factorial design was developed.

TABLE XIII

Number, mean and standard deviation of cells under different combinations of independent variables. Self–concept, (A_1/A_2), achievement motivation (B_1/B_2) and adjustment (C_1/C_2).

Self-Concept

Anxiety is exhibiting the inverse correlation. In interaction also the anxiety is negatively correlated. Hence it is excluded in the above table.

TABLE XIV

Summary Table of Analysis of Variance

Sources of variance	*Sum of Squares*	*Degrees of freedom*	*Mean Squares*	*F1*	*Significance*
A sc	1462.78	1	1462.78	42.39	P<. 05
B AM	3270.98	1	3270.98	94.8	P<. 05
C ADJ	555.25	1	555.25	16.1	P<. 05
AC AM.ADJ	229.76	1	229.76	1	P<. 05
BC AM.ADJ	54.32	1	54.32	1	P<. 05
ABCsc AM.ADJ	608.45	1	608.45	1	P<. 05
ERROR	3134.9	92	36.51		
Total	11499.2	99			

By the researcher with a total of 4 cells. For each cell the number of students, mean and standard deviations were found out, the details of this information are given in the table XIII. Multiple classification of analysis of variance was made use of for the purpose of analyzing the data.

Using the data found in the Table XIII, the expected values of mean squares were derived with the help pf computer; the summary table of analysis of variance is presented in the table XIV.

The data found in the table XIV has been made use of for testing the various hypothesis stated in the previous chapter, the details of testing of each hypothesis and its interpretation. Are discussed in the pages to follow.

Self-Concept and Anxiety

Hypotheses related to self-concept, anxiety and academic achievement of physically handicapped students of 9th std, are:

1. There is no significant difference in respect of the mean scores of physically handicapped children belonging to high self-concept and low self-concept groups.
2. There is no significant difference in respect of the mean scores of academic achievement of physically handicapped children belonging to high anxiety and the low anxiety group.
3. There is no significant difference in the interaction between self-concept and anxiety on academic achievement.

TABLE XV

Mean and Standard Deviation for the Academic Achievement Scores of 2 Levels of Self-concept and Anxiety Groups.

	High self-concept	*Low self-concept*	*High Anxiety*	*Low anxiety*
MEAN	68.8	57.6	60.0	65.1
S.D.	9.88	8.87	8.41	13.42

To test the above hypothesis, data found in the table XV was used. The table XV presents the mean and standard deviation of scores of academic Achievement of high self-concept and low self-concept groups. They were found to be 68.8, 9.88 and 8.87 respectively. The mean and standard deviation of achievement scores of high and low anxiety groups were found to be 60.0 and 65.1 and S.D. of 8.41 and 13.42 respectively. The mean difference of achievement scores of high self-concept and low self-concept was 11.2. This mean difference has to be tested for its significance, likewise the mean difference of achievement scores of high and low anxiety groups was a 5.1 to test these two hypothesis of variance was used. The results obtained by the analysis are presented in Table XVI.

TABLE XVI

Summary Table of Analysis of Variance for the Achievement Scores of 2 Levels of Self-Concept and Anxiety Groups

Sources of Variance	*SS*	*DF*	*MSS*	*F*	*Significance*
Between self-concept	2925.6	1	2925.6	36.8	P<. 05
Between anxiety	701.9	1	701.9	8.8	P<. 05
interaction	100.7	1	100.7	1.3	P<. 05
With in the group	7636.2	96	79.49		
Total	113592	99			

1. Hypothesis

There is no significant difference in respect of the mean scores of academic achievement of physically handicapped children belonging to high self-concept and low self-concept groups.

To test the above hypothesis, the data found in the tables XV & XVI has been made use of, using multiple classification of analysis of variance tested the hypothesis.

The obtained 'F' value of 36.8 was found to be significant at 0.05 level of significance. Hence, the null hypothesis that is no significant difference in the scores of academic achievement of students of high self-concept and low self-concept groups was rejected.

The rejection of the hypothesis indicates that there is significant difference in the mean scores of academic achievement of high and low self-concept groups.

The mean achievement scores of high and low self-concept groups were 68.8 and 59.6 respectively. It was further found that the mean difference of 11.2 was found to be favour of high self-concept group there by indicating that the high self-concept group performed better than the low self-concept group.

From this it could be inferred that the anxiety affects the performance of the students. That is, higher the self-concept higher will be the academic achievement.

The results found in this study were in conformity of the results reported by Michael (1085) and Harvey David (1984).

2. *Hypothesis*

There is no significant differences in respect of the mean scores of the academic achievement of physically handicapped children belonging to high anxiety and low anxiety groups.

To test the above hypothesis, the data found in Table XV & XVI has been made use of the hypothesis, was tested by using multiple classification of analysis of variance.

The obtained 'F' value of 8.8 was found to be significant At 0.05 level of significance. Hence the null hypothesis that there is no significant difference in the scores of academic achievement of students of high anxiety and low anxiety groups was rejected.

The rejection of.hypothesis indicates that there is significant difference in the mean scores of academic achievement of High Anxiety and Low Anxiety groups.

The mean achievement scores of High Anxiety and Low Anxiety groups were 60.0 and 65.1 respectively. It was further found that the mean difference of 5.1' was found to be in favour of Low Anxiety groups. There by indicating that the low Anxiety group has performed better than the High Anxiety groups. From this it could be inferred that the Anxiety higher will be the achievement. The result found in this study was in conformity of the results reported by Mehrotra (1986).

3. *Hypothysis*

There is no significant interaction between self-concept and Anxiety on an academic achievement.

To test the above hypothesis, the data found in table XVI has been made use of. The obtained 'F' value of 1.3 was found to be non-significant at 0.05 level of significant. Hence the null hypothesis that there is no significant interaction between self-concept and Anxiety on Academic Achievement was accepted. The acceptance of hypothesis indicates, that there is no significant interaction between self-concept and anxiety on academic achievement. From this it could be concluded that self-concept and anxiety together will not have any effect on academic achievement of the students.

Self-concept and Achievement Motivation

Hypotheses related to self-concept, achievement motivations and academic achievement of physically handicapped students of IXth standard are:

4. *Hypothesis*

(4). There is no significant difference in the, mean scores of academic achievement of physically handicapped children belonging to high achievement motivation and low achievement motivation groups.

(5). There is no significant difference in respect of the mean scores of academic achievement of physically handicapped children belonging to high self-concept and low self-concept groups.

(6). There is no significant interaction between self-concept and achievement motivation on academic achievement.

TABLE XVII

Mean and Standard Deviations for the Academic Achievement Scores of 2 Levels of Achievement Motivation and Self-Concept

	High ach. Mot.	*Low ach. mot*	*High self concept*	*Low self concept*
Mean	74.7	56.7	68.8	57.6
S.D.	7.90	6.74	9.38	8.87

To test the above hypotheses, data found in table XVII was used. Table XVII presents the mean and standard deviation of scores of academic achievement of high achievement motivation and low achievement motivation groups. They were found to be 74.7, 56.7, standard deviation 7.90 and 6.74 respectively. The mean and standard deviation of scores of academic achievement of high and low self-concept groups were found to be 68.8 and 57.6 respectively and standard deviation of 9.88 and 8.87 respectively. The mean difference of achievement scores of high achievement motivation and low achievement motivation was 18.0. This mean difference has to be tested for its significance. Likewise the mean difference of achievement scores high and low self-concept groups was 11.2. To test these two hypotheses and also hypothesis related to interaction of these variables, multiple classification of analysis of variance was used. The results obtained by the analysis are presented in Table XVII.I.

Hypothesis

(4) There is no significant difference in respect of the mean scores of academic achievement of physically

handicapped children belonging to high achievement motivation and low achievement motivation groups.

TABLE XVIII

Summary Table of Analysis of Variance of the Achievement Scores of 2 Levels of Achievement Motivation and Self-concept Groups

Sl. No.	*Sources of variance*	*SS*	*DF*	*MSS*	*F*	*Significance*
1.	Between ach. Mot.	3559.1	1	3359.1	76.2	P<.05
2.	Between self concept	2740.9	1	2740.9	58.07	P<.05
3.	Interaction	718.5	1	718.5	15.04	P<.05
4.	Within the group	4480.2	96	46.7		
	Total	11499.2	99			

To test the above hypothesis, the data found in table XVII & XVIII has been made use of, using multiple classification of analysis of variance tested the hypothesis.

The obtained 'F' value of 76.2 was found to be significant at 0.05 level of significance. Hence the null hypothesis that there is no significant difference in the scores of academic achievement of students of high achievement motivation and low achievement motivation groups was rejected. The rejection of hypothesis indicates that there is a significant difference in the mean scores of academic achievement of physically handicapped children belonging to high and low motivated groups.

The mean achievement scores of high and low achievement motivated groups were 74.7& 56.7 respectively. It was further found that the mean difference of 18.0 was found to be in favour of high motivated group, there by indicating that, the high achievement groups, has performed better than the low motivated groups, motivation affects the performance of the students, that is, higher the motivation, higher will be the achievement.

5. Hypothesis

There is no significant difference in respect of the mean scores of the academic achievement of physically handicapped children belonging to high self-concept and low self-concept groups.

To test the above hypothesis, the data found in the table XVII&XVIII has been made use of, using multiple classification of analysis of variance tested the hypothesis.

The obtained 'F' value of 58.7 was found to be significant at 0.05 level of significance. Hence the null hypothesis that there is no significant difference in the academic achievement of high self-concept and low self-concept groups was rejected.

The rejection of hypothesis indicates that there is significant difference in the scores of achievement of high and low self-concept groups.

The achievement scores of high and low self-concept were 68.8 &57.6 respectively. It was found that the mean difference of 11.2 was found to be in favour of high self-concept group. There by indicating that the high self-concept group has performed better than the low self concept group. From this it could be inferred that the self-concept higher will be achievement. The results found in this study was in conformity of the results reported by Padhi (1990).

6. Hypothesis

There is no significant interaction between achievement motivation and self-concept on the scores of academic achievement.

To test the above hypothesis was tested by using multiple classification of analysis of variance.

The obtained 'F value of 15.4 was found to be significant at .05 level of significance. Hence the null hypothesis that there is no significant interaction between achievement motivation and self-concept on the scores of academic achievement was rejected.

The rejection of hypothesis indicates that there is significant interaction between achievement motivation and self-concept on academic achievement. From this it could be concluded that achievement motivation and self-concept together will have an effect on scores of academic achievement of the students. The results found in this study was in conformity of the results reported by Mamatha (1992).

Self-Concept and Adjustment

Hypotheses related to self-concept, adjustment and academic achievement of physically handicapped students of 9th standard are,

Hypothesis

(7) There is no significant difference in respect of the scores of academic achievement of physically handicapped children of high self-concept and low self-concept groups.

(8). There is no significant difference in respect of the scores of academic achievement of physically handicapped children belonging to high adjustment and low adjustment groups.

(9). There is no significant interaction between self- concept and adjustment on academic achievement.

To test the above hypothesis, the data found in table XIX was used. Table XIX presents the mean standard deviation of scores of academic achievement of high self-concept and low self-concept groups. They were found to be 68.8 and57.6 respectively and 9.88 and 8.87 respectively. The mean and standard deviation on achievement scores of high adjustment and low adjustment groups were found to be 70.0 and 57.9

TABLE XIX

Mean and Standard Deviation for the Academic Achievement Scores of 2 Levels of Self- Concept and Adjustment Groups

	High Self - Concept	*Low Self - Concept*	*High Adjustment*	*Low Adjustment*
Mean	68.8	57.6	70.3	57.9
S.D.	9.88	8.87	10.10	8.54

TABLE XX

Summary Table of Analysis of Variance of the Achievement Scores of 2 Levels of Self-Concept and Adjustment Groups

Sl. No	*Sources*	*SS*	*DF*	*MSS*	*F*	*Significant*
1.	Between Self-Concept	1818.2	1	1818.2	28.4	P<.05
2.	Between Adjustment	3381.9	1	3381.9	52.9	P<.05
3.	Interaction Between SC & Adj	266.9	1	266.9	4.1	P<.05
4.	Within the group	6037.1	96	63.9		
	Total	11497.2	99			

and S.D. of 10.10 and 8.54 respectively. The mean difference of high self-concept and low self-concept was 11.2. This mean difference has to be tested for its significance likewise the mean difference of achievement scores of high and low adjustment groups was 12.4. To test these two hypotheses and also the hypothesis related to interaction of these variables, multiple classification of analysis of variance was used. The results obtained by the analysis are presented in table XX.

Hypothesis

7. There is no significant difference in respect of the mean scores of academic achievement of physically handicapped children belonging to high self-concept and low self-concept groups.

To test the above hypothesis, the data found in table XIX and XX has been made use of, the hypothesis was tested by using multiple classification of analysis of variance.

The obtained 'F' value of 28.4 was found to be significant at 0.05 level of significance. Hence the null hypothesis that there is no significant difference in the academic achievement of high self-concept and low self-concept groups was rejected.

The rejection of hypothesis indicates that there is significant difference in the academic achievement of physically handicapped children belonging to high self-concept and low self-concept groups.

The mean achievement scores of high and low self-concept groups were 68.8 and 57.6 respectively. It was further found that the mean difference of 11.2 was found to be in favour of high self-concept group, there by indicating that the high self-concept group has performed well than the low self-concept group. From this it could be inferred that, the self-concept affects the performance of the students, that is higher the self-concept higher will be the achievement.

8. Hypothesis

There is no significant difference in respect of the mean scores of academic achievement of physically handicapped children belonging to high adjustment and low adjustment groups.

To test the above hypothesis the data found in the table XIX and XX has been made use. The hypothesis was tested by using multiple classification of analysis of variance.

The obtained 'F' value of 52.9 was found to be significant at 0.05 level of significance. Hence the null hypothesis that there is no significant difference in the scores of academic achievement of high adjustment and low adjustment groups was rejected.

The rejection of hypothesis indicates that there is a significant difference in the academic achievement of high adjustment and low adjustment groups.

The mean achievement scores of high and low adjusted groups were 70.3 and 57.9 respectively. It was further found that the mean difference of 12.4 was found to be in favour of high-adjusted group, there by indicating that the high-adjusted group has performed well than the low adjusted group. From this it could be conformed that the adjustment also affects the performance of the students, that is higher the adjustment higher will be the achievement. The results found in this study was in conformity of the results reported by Mehrotran(1986).

Hypothesis

9. There is no significant interaction between self-concept and adjustment on scores of academic achievement.

To rest the above hypothesis, the data found in the table XX has been made use of; the hypothesis was tested by using multiple classification of analysis of variance.

The obtained 'F' value of 4.1 was found to be significant at 0.05 level of the significance. Hence the null hypothesis that there is no significant interaction between self-concept and adjustment of scores of academic achievement was rejected. The rejection of hypothesis indicates that, there is a significant interaction between self-concept and adjustment on academic achievement.

Anxiety and Achievement Motivation

Hypothesis related to anxiety and achievement motivation on academic achievement of physically handicapped students of 9th std. are

10. There is no significant difference in respect of the mean scores of academic achievement of physically handicapped children belonging to high anxiety groups.

11. There is no significant difference in respect of the mean scores of academic achievement of physically handicapped children belonging to high achievement motivation and low achievement motivation groups.

12. There is no significant difference in the interaction between anxiety and achievement motivation on academic achievement.

TABLE XXI

Mean and Standard Deviation for the Academic Achievement Scores of 2 Level of Anxiety and Achievement Motivation

	High anxiety	*Low anxiety*	*High ach. Motivation*	*Low ach. Motivation*
Mean	60.0	65.1	74.7	56.7
S.D.	8.41	13.42	7.90	6.74

To test the above hypothesis, data found in the table XXI was used. Table XXI presents the mean and standard deviation of scores of academic achievement of high anxiety and low anxiety groups. These were found to be 60.0, 65.1 and S.D. of 8.41, 13.42 respectively. The mean and standard deviation of achievement scores of high and low achievement motivation was found to be 74.7 and 56.7 and S.D. of 7.90,6.74 respectively. The mean difference of high anxiety and low anxiety was 5.1. The mean difference has to be tested for its significance. Like wise the mean difference of achievement scores of high and low achievement motivation groups was 18.0 to test these two hypotheses and also the interaction of these variable. Multiple classification of analysis of variance was used. The results obtained by the analysis are found in table XXII.

TABLE XXII

Summary Table of Analysis of Variance for the Achievement Scores of 2 Levels of Anxiety & Achievement Motivation

Sources of Variance	*Sum of Square*	*DF*	*Mean Sum of Square*	*F*	*Significance*
Betn. anxiety	777.2	1	777.2	18.0	P< .05 sig
Betn. Ach.Mot	6541.9	1	6541.9	158.0	P< .05 sig
Interaction Betn.Ach.Mot	78.0	1	78.0	1.9	Ps
Within group	4102.9	96	41.4	—	—
Total	11499.2	99	—	—	—

10. Hypothesis

There is no significant difference in respect of the Mean scores of academic achievement of physically handicapped children belonging to high anxiety and low anxiety groups.

To test the above hypothesis, the data found in the table XXI and XXII has been made use of the hypothesis, was tested by using multiple classification of analysis of variance.

The obtained 'f' value of 18.8 was found to be significant at 0.05 level of significance. Hence the null hypothesis that there is no significant difference in the scores of academic achievement of high anxiety and low anxiety groups was rejected. The rejection of hypothesis indicates that three is significant difference in the scores of academic achievement of high anxiety and low anxiety groups.

The mean achievement scores of high and low anxiety groups were 6.0 and 65.1 respectively. It was further found that the mean difference of 5.1 was found to be in favour of low anxiety groups.

Thereby it indicates that the low anxiety group has performed better than the high anxiety group. From this it could be inferred that the anxiety affects the performance of the students, that is lower the anxiety higher will be the achievement.

11. Hypothesis

There is no significant difference in respect of the mean scores of academic achievement of physically handicaped children belonging to high achievement motivation and low achievement motivation groups.

To test the above hypothesis, the data found in the table XXI and XXII has been made use of, using multiple classification of analysis of variance tested the hypothesis.

The obtained 'F'value of 15.8 was found to be significant at 0.05 level of significance. Hence the null hypothesis that there is no significant difference in high achievement motivation and low achievement motivation groups was rejected. The rejection of hypothesis indicates that there is a significant difference in the achievement of high and low motivated groups.

The mean achievement scores of high and motivated group were 74.7 and 56.7 respectively. It was further found that the mean difference of 18 was found to be in favour of high-motivated groups, there by indicating that the high-motivated group has performed better than the low motivated group. From this it could be inferred that the motivation affects the performance of the students that is, higher will be the achievement. The results found in this study was in conformity with the results reported by Shan mugs Sundaram (1983) Deshpande (1984), Sween (1984), Mitra (1985)

12. Hypothesis

There is no significant interaction between anxiety and achievement motivation on the mean scores of academic achievement.

To test the above hypothesis the data found in the table XXII has been made use of, the hypothesis was tested by using multiple classification of analysis of variance.

The obtained 'F' value of 1.9 was found to be non significant at 0.05 level of significance.

Hence the null hypothesis that there is no significant interaction between anxiety and achievement motivation on academic achievement was accepted. The acceptance of hypothesis indicates that there is no significant interaction between anxiety and achievement motivation on scores of academic achievement.

From this it could be concluded that anxiety and achievement motivation together will not have any effect on the scores of academic achievement of the student.

Anxiety and Adjustment

The hypothesis related to anxiety, adjustment and academic achievement of physically handicapped students of 9th standard are:

13. There is no significant difference in respect of the mean scores of academic achievement of physically handicapped children belonging to high anxiety and low anxiety groups.

14. There is no significant difference in respect of the mean scores of academic achievement of physically handicapped children belonging to high adjustment and low adjustment groups.

15. There is no significant interaction between anxiety and adjustment on academic and adjustment.

TABLE XXIII

Mean and Standard Deviation for the Academic Achievement of 2 Levels of Anxiety and Adjustment

	High anxiety	*Low anxiety*	*High Adjustment*	*Low Adjustment*
Mean	60.0	65.1	70.3	57.9
S.D	8.41	13.4	10.10	6.54

To test the above hypothesis, data found in table XXIII was used. Table XXIII presents the mean and standard deviation of scores of academic achievement of high anxiety and low anxiety groups. They were found to be 60.0, 65.1 and S.D. of 8.41 and 13.42 respectively. The mean difference of high anxiety and low anxiety was 5.1. The mean difference has to be tested for its significance. Like wise the mean and standard deviation of high and low adjustment were found to be 70.3, 57..9, and S.D. of 10.10 and 8.54 respectively. The mean difference of high and low adjustment was 12.4 to test these two hypotheses and also the interaction of these variables. Multiple classification of analysis of variance was used. The results obtained by the analysis were found in table XXIV.

TABLE XXIV

Summary Table of Analysis of Variance of the Achievement of 2 Levels of Anxiety and Adjustment

Sources of Variance Square	*Sum of*	*DF of Square*	*Mean Sum*	*F*	*Significance*
Betn.anxiety	1007.7	1	1007.7	11.9	P< .05 sig
Betn.Adjust.	3403.6	1	3403:6	402	P< .05 sig
Interaction Betn.Ach.Adj.	101.7	1	101.7	1.20	Ns
Within group	8131.2	96		84.7	—
Total	12644.2	99	—	—	—

13. Hypothesis

There is no significant difference in the mean scores of academic achievement of high anxiety and low anxiety groups.

To test the above hypothesis, the data found in table XXIII and XXIV has been made use of, using multiple classification of analysis of variance tested the hypothesis.

The obtained 'F' value of 11.9 was found to be significant at 0.05 level of significance. Hence the null hypothesis that there is no significant difference in the mean scores of academic achievement of high anxiety and low anxiety groups was rejected.

The rejection of hypothesis indicates that there is significant difference in the scores of academic achievement of high anxiety and low anxiety groups.

The mean achievement scores of high and low anxiety groups were found to be 60.0 and 65.1 was found to be in favour of low anxiety group. Thereby indicating that the low anxiety group has performed better than the high anxiety group. From this is it could be inferred that the anxiety affects the performance of the students. That is lower the anxiety higher will be the achievement.

14. Hypothesis

There is no significant difference in respect of the mean scores of academic achievement of physically handicapped children belonging to high adjustment and low adjustment groups.

To test the above hypothesis, the data found in the table XXIII and XXIV has been made use of. Using multiple classification of analysis of variance tested the hypothesis.

The obtained 'F' value of 40.2 was found to be significant at 0.05 level of significance. Hence the null hypothesis that there is no significant difference in the academic achievement of high adjustment and low adjustment groups was rejected.

The rejection of hypothesis indicates that there is significant difference in the scores of academic achievement of high adjustment and low adjustment groups.

The mean achievement scores of high and low adjustment groups were 70.3 and 57.9 respectively. It was further found that the mean difference of 12.4 was found to be in favour of high-adjusted groups, thereby indicating that the high-adjusted group has performed better than the low adjusted group. From this it could be inferred that the adjustment also affects the performance of the students, that is higher the adjustment higher will be the achievement.

15. Hypothesis

There is no significant interaction between anxiety and adjustment on academic achievement.

To test the above hypothesis, the data found in the table XXIV has been made use of; using multiple classification of analysis of variance tested the hypothesis.

The obtained 'F' value of 120 was found to be non significant at 0.05 level of significance. Hence the null hypothesis that there is no significant interaction between anxiety and adjustment on the scores of academic achievement was accepted. The acceptance of hypothesis indicates that there is no significant interaction between anxiety and adjustment on the scores of academic achievement.

From this it could be concluded that, anxiety and adjustment together will not have any effect on the scores of academic achievement of the students. The results found in this study were in conformity with the results reported by Mohanty (1985), Allen Elizabeth (1980).

Achievement Motivation and Adjustment

The hypotheses related to achievement motivation, adjustment and academic achievement of physically handicapped children of 9th standard are:

16. There is no significant difference in respect of the mean scores of academic achievement of physically handicapped children belonging to high achievement motivation and low achievement motivation groups.

17. There is no significant difference in respect of the mean scores of academic achievement of physically handicapped children belonging to high adjustment and low adjustment groups.

18. There is no significant interaction between achievement motivation and adjustment on academic achievement.

TABLE XXV

Mean and Standard Deviation for the Academic Achievement of 2 Levels of Achievements Motivation and Adjustment

	High ach.mot.	*Low ach.ot.*	*High Adjustment*	*Low Adjustment*
Mean	74.7	56.7	70.3	57.9
S.D	7.90	6.74	10.10	8.54

To test the above hypothesis, the data found in the table XXV was used. Table XXV presents the mean and standard deviation of high achievement motivation and low achievement motivation were found to be 74.7, 56.7S.D.of 7.90 & 6.74 respectively. The mean and standard deviation of achievement scores of high and low adjustment were found to be 70.3, 57.9, and S.D. of 10.10 and 8.54 respectively. The mean difference of high achievement motivation and low achievement motivation was 18.0. The mean difference has to be tested for its significance, like wise the mean difference of high and low adjustment group was 12.4.

To test these two hypotheses and also the hypothesis related to interaction of these two variables, multiple classification of analysis of variance was used. The results obtained by the analysis are presented in Table XXVI.

TABLE XXVI

Summary Table of Analysis of Variance for the Achievement of 2 Levels of Achievement Motivation and Adjustment

Sources of Variance	*Sum of Square*	*DF*	*Mean Sum of Square*	*F*	*Significance*
Betn. ach.mot.	3391.8	1	3391.8	74.05	P< .05 sig
Betn.Adjust.	3401.0	1	3401.0	74.3	P< .05 sig
Interaction Betn. Ach.mot.Adj	417.4	1	417.4	9.10	P< .05 sig
Within group	4394.0	96			
Total	11606.2	99			

16. Hypothesis

There is no significant difference in respect of the mean scores of academic achievement of physically handicapped children belonging to high achievement motivation and low achievement motivation groups.

To test the above hypothesis, the data found in the table XXV and XXVII has been made use of, using multiple classification of analysis of variance tested the hypothesis.

The obtained 'F' value of 74.05 was found to be significant at 0.05 level of significance. Hence the null hypothesis that there is no significant difference in the high achievement motivation and low achievement motivation groups was rejected. The rejection of hypothesis indicates that there is a significant difference in the scores of achievement of high and low motivated groups.

The mean achievement score of high and low motivated groups were found to be 74.7 respectively. It was further found that the mean difference of 18.0 was found to be in favour of high-motivated group. There by indicating that the high motivated group has performed better than the low motivated group. From this it could be inferred that the adjustment also affects the performance of the students, that is higher the adjustment higher will be the achievement. The results found in this study were in conformity with the results reported by Indrani (1985).

17. Hypothesis

There is no significant difference in respect of the mean scores of academic achievement of physically handicapped children belonging to high adjustment and low adjustment groups.

To test the above hypothesis, the data was tested by using multiple classification of analysis of variance.

The obtained 'F' value of 74.3 was found to be significant at 0.05 level of significance. Hence the null hypothesis that there is no significant difference in the academic achievement of high adjustment and low adjustment group was rejected.

The rejection of hypothesis indicates that there is a significant difference in the academic achievement of high adjustment and low adjustment groups.

The mean achievement scores of high and low adjusted groups are 70.3 and 57.9 respectively. It was further found that the mean difference of 12.4 was found to be in favours of high-adjusted groups. Thereby indicating that the high-adjusted group performed better than the low adjusted group. From this it could be inferred that the adjustment also affects the performance of the students, that is higher the adjustment higher will be the achievement.

18. Hypothesis

There is no significant interaction between achievement motivation and adjustment on academic achievement.

To test the above hypothesis, the data found in the table XXVI has been made use of; using multiple classification of analysis of variance tested the hypothesis.

The obtained 'F' value of 9.1 was found to be significant at0.05 level of significance. Hence the null hypothesis that there is no significant interaction between achievement motivation and adjustment on academic achievement was rejected. The rejection of hypothesis indicates that there is significant interaction between achievement motivation and adjustment on academic achievement.

From this it could be concluded that achievement motivation and adjustment together will have effect on the scores of academic achievement of the students.

General Conclusion

Thus it is concluded that self-concept, low anxiety high achievement motivation and well adjustment helps to attain a better academic achievement and a good adjustment among the physically handicapped students.

So far, a detailed discussion about the hypotheses has been presented. In order to give quick information about the acceptance and rejection of the hypotheses, a table consisting of hypotheses, 'F' values, and the decision taken is presented in table XXVII.

5

Summary and Conclusion

SUMMARY

In the previous chapter, the analysis and interpretation of data was presented in detail. In this chapter, the researcher presents a brief summary of the research, which includes the variables, objectives, hypotheses, tools, methodology, conclusions, educational implications, limitations of the study and suggestions for further study.

Children of any school or of any country are depending on their scholastic achievement as above average, average, or normal and below average. Majority of the children come under the category of average or normal. There are few children who may be found to deviate mentally, socially, scholastically and physically from the normal children. These deviated children are designated as exceptional children.

In the present study, the researcher has chosen only the physically handicapped (crippled) children. These children come under the group of exceptional children. Physical handicapped children are those children who has the physical disability like muscular dystrophy, impairment in the joints of bones, osteomyelities, poliomyelitis, paralysis, cerebral palsy, club foot, Epilepsy, multiple sclerosis etc. Because of these deformities, these children suffer from coping problems more than the normal children. The coping problems faced by these children are as intervertedness, pessimistic attitude, emotional instability, passive, self-centered, anxiety ridden, helplessness, lack of self- concept and lack of achievement motivation. To overcome these – coping problems and to meet the unique needs these children need special education?

Kothari Education Commission (1964-66) has suggested that the education of the physically handicapped children is to be organized not merely on humanitarian grounds, but also on utilitarian grounds. Proper education makes handicapped children enable to overcome there handicaps and make them acceptable and useful citizens of the society.

Dependent and independent variables are considered in the study.

Independent variables are:

1. Self-concept (Sc)
2. Anxiety (An)
3. Achievement motivation (Am).
4. Adjustment (Adj)

Dependent variable is Academic Achievement (AA).

Objectives of the Study

The following objectives have been formulated to assess:

1. The academic achievement of physically handicapped children of high and low self-concept group.
2. The academic achievement of physically handicapped children of high and low anxiety group.
3. The significance difference in the interaction between self-concept and anxiety on academic achievement.

4. The academic achievement of physically handicapped children of high and low achievement motivation group.
5. The academic achievement of physically handicapped children of high and low self-concept group.
6. The significance difference in the interaction between achievement motivation and self-concept on academic achievement.
7. The academic achievement of physically handicapped children of high and low adjustment group.
8. The academic achievement of physically handicapped children of high and low self-concept group.
9. The significance in the interaction between adjustment and self-concept on academic achievement.
10. The academic achievement of physically handicapped children of high and low anxiety group.
11. The academic achievement of physically handicapped children of high and low achievement motivation group.
12. The significance difference in the interaction between anxiety and achievement motivation on academic achievement
13. The academic achievement of physically handicapped children of high and low anxiety group.
14. The academic achievement of physically handicapped children of high and low adjustment group.

15. The significance difference in the interaction between anxiety and adjustment on academic achievement.
16. The academic achievement of physically handicapped children of high and low achievement motivation group.
17. The academic achievement of physically handicapped children belonging to high and low adjustment group.
18. The significance difference in the interaction between achievement motivation and adjustment on academic achievement.
19. To construct an adjustment inventory to identify their adjustment
20. Construct an achievement test for the IX STD to measure their achievement.

Hypothesis

In pursuance of the specific objectives stated above, the following hypotheses were set-up.

1. There is no significant difference in respect of the mean scores of academic achievement of physically handicapped children belonging to high self-concept and low self- concept groups.
2. There is n o significant difference in respect of the mean scores of academic achievement of physically handicapped children belonging to high anxiety and low anxiety groups.
3. There is no significant difference in the interaction between self- concept and anxiety on academic achievement.
4. There is no significant difference in respect of the mean scores of academic achievement of physically

handicapped children belonging to high and low achievement motivation groups.

5. There is no significant difference in respect of the mean scores of academic achievement of physically handicapped children belonging to high and low self-concept groups.
6. There is no significant difference in the interaction between self-concept and achievement motivation on an academic achievement.
7. There is no significant difference in respect of the mean scores of academic achievement of physically handicapped children belonging to high and low adjustment groups.
8. There is no significant difference in respect of the mean scores of academic achievement of physically handicapped children belonging to high and low self-concept groups.
9. There is no significant difference in the interaction between self-concept and adjustment on academic achievement.

   There is no significant difference in respect of the mean scores of academic achievement of physically handicapped children
10. There is no significant difference in respect of the mean scores of academic achievement of physically handicapped children belonging to high and low achievement motivation groups.
11. There is no significant difference in the interaction between anxiety and achievement motivation on academic achievement.
12. There is no significant difference in respect of the mean scores of academic achievement of physically

handicapped children belonging to high and low anxiety groups.

13. There is no significant difference in respect of the mean scores of academic achievement of physically handicapped children belonging to high and low adjustment groups.
14. There is no significant difference in the interaction between anxiety and adjustment on academic achievement.
15. There is no significant difference in respect of the mean scores of academic achievement of physically handicapped children belonging to high and low achievement motivation groups.
16. There is no significant difference in the mean scores of academic achievement of physically handicapped children belonging to high and low adjustment groups.
17. There is no significant difference in the interaction between achievement motivation and adjustment on the Scores of academic achievement

Methodology

The success of any research study depends on the selection and utilization of proper research methods. Methods selected should be feasible, preplanned, well understood and should always be appropriate to the problem under investigation and the kind of data necessary for its solution.

In educational research there are various methods such as experimental method, descriptive method, historical method etc.

For the present study the descriptive method was used. The descriptive method is designed to obtain pertinent and precise information concerning the current status of phenomena and whenever possible to draw valid general conclusions from the facts discovered.

Tools Used for Collection of Data

The following tools were used for the collection of data.

1. Vasantha Ramkumar -q-sort set for measuring self-concept.
2. Sinha's manifest anxiety scale for measuring anxiety
3. Dee Mohan's achievement motivation scale for measuring achievement motivation.
4. Adjustment inventory constructed by the researcher to find out the adjusting problems of the children's.
5. Achievement test –constructed by the researcher was used to measure the academic achievement of the students.

Sample

100 children were selected for the study on the basis of random sampling technique from the schools of the three-district Chitradurga, Dharwad and Bellary in Karnataka state.

The main aim of the present investigation was to explore the relationship between independent variable such as self-concept, anxiety, and achievement motivation and also to see impact of the interaction of two variables on academic achievement.

Statistical Techniques

Multiple classification of analysis of variance was used to test the significance of hypothesis.

CONCLUSIONS

Based upon the discussion and interpretation of the data the researcher arrived at the following conclusions:

1. The self-concept affects the performance of the children, that is higher the self-concept higher will be the academic achievement
2. The anxiety affects the performance of the children, that is lower the anxiety higher will be the achievement.
3. The self-concept and anxiety together will not have any effect on academic achievement.
4. The motivation affects the performance of the children that is higher the motivation higher will be the achievement.
5. Self- concept affects the performance of the children. Higher the self-concept higher will be the achievement.
6. Achievement motivation and self- concept together will have effect on academic achievement; there is an interaction between them.
7. Self-concept affects the performance of the children higher the self-concept higher will be the achievement.
8. The adjustment also affects the performance of the children that is higher the adjustment higher will be the achievement.
9. The self-concept and adjustment together will have effect on academic achievement.
10. The Anxiety affects the performance of the children. Lower the anxiety higher will be the achievement.
11. Motivation affects the performance of the children. Higher the motivation higher will be the achievement.
12. Anxiety and achievement motivation together does not have any effect on academic achievement of the children.

13. Anxiety affects the performance of the children. Higher the anxiety, lower will be the achievement.
14. Adjustment affects the performance of the children. Higher the adjustment higher will be the achievement.
15. Anxiety and adjustment together does not have any effect on academic achievement.
16. Motivation affects the performance of the children, that is higher the motivation higher will be the achievement.
17. Adjustment also affects the performance of the children, that is higher the adjustment higher will be the achievement.
18. Achievement motivation and adjustment together will Have effect on academic achievement.

EDUCATIONAL IMPLICATION

Education has been regarded as a matter of primary national importance. The major objective of modern education is to develop well-informed and intellectually active citizens. To educate its citizens, schemes like universal free and compulsory education have been introduced in our country.

In school, maladjustment not only creates problems to the teacher but also they spoil the school. They have created widespread problems of social indiscipline, due to the personal suffering. This in turn leads loss to the society. The youthful power is not properly tapped for social, cultural and economic betterment, so the problem of adjustment has become an important issue that no conscious parent can ignore it.

From the early periods educators and counseling psychologists alike have recognized the value and need to consider children's self-concept as an educationally significant variable, students self-concept is also important in understanding the dynamics of other features of classroom teaching etc. like interaction of success and self-image. Influence of student's participation and learning. Self-concept has been shown to operate with some independence in various parts roles of person's life such as school, work, relationships, family life and religion. The factors of particular interest in understanding self-concept in school settings are academic interest in children's self-concept is an important consideration because it is substantially related to academic achievement. The association of positive self-concept with academic achievement has been found to be true. Findings from personality research suggest that self-concept is an important aspect in the dynamics of learning and performance. Persons with high self-concept act with confidence on their own best judgment without feeling, guilty, and defend their values (Franklin, 1979, Gurmeet, 1986).

The areas of self-concept, which have significant bearing on academic achievement, are intellectual, social status, physical appearance, and attributes. For developing self-concept of children on their intellectual status, creative work problem, playing games debates, quiz, seminars and group discussion should be introduced on a large scale in school. Due recognition and appreciation in the above activities should be given by awarding prizes and award. Camp and educational excursions can also help in developing group feeling among children. Teachers must help the child to develop self-concept through their approval and interpersonal relations organizations of varied types of functions and extra curricular programmes provide excellent opportunities for sharing responsibilities and thereby gaining a position of status. (Melvin, 1929).

Anxiety is considered as a thwarted behavior of the child. A child who suffers from anxiety may not be able to devote his full energy in the performance of a task. It is therefore considered that anxiety interferes with the anxiety and so learning is impeded (Mathur 1985). One of the important function of the teacher or of any leader is that of reducing anxiety, but some minimum anxiety is essential for learning, but too much anxiety has a disturbing effect in a group, (it arouse hostility and provokes aggressive behavior. Over anxiety prevents individual from seeing the facts as they really are.)

To face anxiety, a child must learn to cope with his own internal condition. His/ her urges, desires or interests are to be fulfilled. In order to have good emotional experiences the favourable environmental conditions should exist in the school. He needs to be helped to understand himself and achieve a degree of self acceptance that enables him to be free as far as its humanly possible from irrational feeling of guilt and other forms of self-disagreement with teacher.

In order to reduce the anxiety, involve the children in the social activities. 1) It helps to keep them away from the fear of being alone. 2) Based on rationalization the child must avoid all situation, thoughts or feelings which creates anxiety, another way of reducing anxiety is to deny its existence. In fact, nothing is done about anxiety in such cases except denying it, which is excluding it from consciousness.

Help the anxious child to prevent or to minimize the provocation that lead to anxiety, praise or the use of a compliment is effective in helping a student to overcome his resentment of a real or fancied hurt, some pleasant remark, even divert the individual away from the state of wrath toward a more wholesome attitude.

In a class room the anxiety may be reduced if the teacher endeavours to keep the general atmosphere of the class cheerful, harmonious and co-operative. If the instruction is interesting, the class work is stimulating, ample provision to be made for engaging extra-curricular activities. The teacher must reduce disharmony between what they practice and what they claim to be their motives and what actually impels them. The teacher must pretend to be democratic but they must be deliberately democratic. We must avoid angry violent and irritating modes of behavior in the classroom at least in order to format the emotional health of his children. Teacher' too, should not show favoritisms or seem to have pets.

Affection is the dominant emotion that he experience in a well adjusted home. He exhibits jealously and varying degrees of resentment if he believes that other members of the family are receiving more attention than he is, to their extent parents need to be impartial and objective in their treatment of the children in the home.

Motivation can be provided to the children by making education child centered. The learning of the child should be judged according to the ability, interest, capacity and previous experiences. The learning material or experiences should always be assigned according to the needs, interest and abilities of the child. The teacher must link the new learning to the past experience. The teacher must use effective methods and devices in teaching. Praise and reproof can be safely used for the achievement and desired motivation in the classroom situation. In the field of education the spirit of competition can be used as a motivating force. Motivation can be enhanced by various ways. Some of them are as follows.

(a) Focusing Children Attention on Desired Objectives

To secure and focus attention, one obvious method is to state clearly the objectives of instructional units as it commences. Much instruction today is ineffective because neither teachers nor children's are aware of exactly what is to be learned. Mager and Clark (1963), and Miles, Kibler and

Pettigrew (1967) have demonstrated that when teachers and children are aware of the objectives. It is more likely that children's attention will be properly focused, and their achievement increased. Another method available to the teacher is to focus attention to stimulate and integrate several sensory modalities in a single presentation or unit. The teacher can appeal to more than one sense, usually both seeing and hearing, often touch, and sometimes smell and taste. Interaction between the teacher and the child, attractive presentation would sustain interest and attention.

(b) Utilizing the Student Needs to Display Competence

There are some clear relationship between the need to display competence over the environment and the need to perform well that is achieved in classrooms. Infact, that the need to achieve can in a sense, be thought of as the need to exhibit competence over a body of subject matter, over a specific skill or task or the like. Further, displaying competence may need to know and understand for esteem. Helping student to satisfy his need is a primary way to develop stable motivation of a high order.

(c) Provide Information Feedback

Students are not always able to evaluate their own responses and usually they need feedback to confirm appropriate or correct responses. Classroom interactions, correction of assignments and programmed learning are generally provided for immediate and usable feedback.

(d) Help Each Student to Set and Attain Appropriate Goals

Goal Setting is Defined as Specifying some state of Affairs — to be attained. We have noted the importance of children having some control over the establishment of their own goals. Goal setting must proceed according to the nature of the taste and the characteristics of the child.

De Charms (1971) Suggested Four Steps to Reach the Required Goals

They are

1. Analyze personal strength and weaknesses.
2. Choose personal goals realistically
3. Select immediate concrete actions that can be taken to move toward the chosen goal.
4. Determine way to tell whether action taken is moving one toward the goal.

(e) Use of Teaching Aids

Real models for student include teachers, and other children at school symbolic models are presented to children through oral or written materials and pictures or through combination of such devices. Representational model presented by audio-visual means, particularly television are also influential. In school considerable attention must be given to exemplary models who demonstrate behavior, initially learned through imitations are strengthened through the use of positive reinforcement.

(f) Use Rewards as Necessary to Secure Desirable Behaviour

Reward given to a child brings satisfaction or pleasure to him. When a child is rewarded immediately after some behavior, learning is strengthened and is likely to secure when the situation is appropriate.

(g) Promote Ego-Involvement

As Sheriffs and Canbril (1979) showed ego-involvement generates the best efforts sustained incentive and purposeful activity. All the strength of the person would be put to good use. It becomes higher levels of personality motives affiliation achievement, competency, esteem and self-actualization. When a given compliments on modes and ways of working and achievement oriented groups performed best in conditions of strong task orientation. Aspiration is also highly motivating but the level of aspiration set should be realization and reasonable other wise the result would be failure and frustration.

A well-adjusted person exhibits a good success in achievement. Whereas the poorly adjusted person exhibits a poor scholastic achievement, they also show some emotional symptoms such as excessive worry, fear, inferiority, hatred, temper tantrum, persistent anxiety, conflicts and tensions.

Maladjusted personality brings misfortune to ones self and discomfort to others therefore it is an urgent necessity to desire some means and takes some precautionary measures in advance. So that we may have well adjusted personalities.

The following measures may be involved to help the children in being better adjusted. We must be careful in bringing balanced growth and development. His physical and mental as well as his social, emotional development should be properly attended to.

Parents must provide opportunities and give necessary assistance to the individual for the satisfaction of basic needs (security recognition, material gains, status etc). Sometimes

Inadequate development of certain needs result in non-adjustive behavior. The degree of ones adjustment is proportional to ones feeling to satisfaction with regard to ones varying needs. The individual should not suffer from physical mental emotional and social starvation.

The individual should be helped in realizing his strengths as well as weaknesses. The individual should be helped in developing tolerance, so that they may break under stresses and strains of the odds of life. Teacher and parents should themselves try to practice the right ways and good habits by themselves. Mere teaching the individual should be made to realize the importance of the culture and social milieu. Proper care should be taken to provide healthy environment for the individuals by the teacher, parents and other responsible members of the society. They should provide an adequate care and love to them and arrange for the satisfaction of their needs as well as actualization of their potentialities. Maladjestment will develop due to faulty, up bringing and counseling services in the school for helping children in making adjustment with their problems.

The role of parents and teachers is very important. Genuine efforts must be made to assist the children to the maximum extent possible to accept their handicaps, be self-reliant and adjust to their limitations. The teacher must collect family background of every crippled child. Teachers should see that these children are provided with recreation facilities, very often, the recreational needs of these children are ignored in the school because of their disability. The parents and teachers may take action to provide relevant aid for mobility of the limbs and functioning of the extremities. The National Policy of Education (1986) has suggested the following measures for the education of the handicapped children. In every district where a special school is set up; a vocational training center would also be developed. Vocational training center provide opportunities to the student to choose the vocations of their interest. Special care is taken for training the craftsman for locally available jobs. Separate hostel facilities are also to be provided for the boys and girls.

Besides teacher's psychologists and educators in each district need to be specially trained for the task of assessment and rehabilitation of the handicapped children, orientation programmes for medical staff, physiotherapists, occupational therapists may also be arranged. Programmes of learning may be done with the health and welfare Ministry (Chintamanikar, 1992). The NPE has suggested "grants to special schools should be given on the basis as the regular schools with adequate provisions to meet the special needs of the disabled children". These handicapped children should be helped in securing job is the responsibility of the Government as well as of society. The Government of India has proposed to provide crores (124) of rupees to the Social Welfare Department for Projects of the handicapped. Vocational rehabilitation centers have also been opened to give special training. The functions of these centers have also been opened to give special training. The functions of these centers: 1) to train them in such units as clerical jobs, Commerce, Drawing and Painting, cutting and tailoring, carpentry, according to ability. 2) To arrange training for proper Vocation of each handicapped who attends the center and to provide them Government scholarships. 3) To make arrangement for the unskilled work through handicapped rehabilitation centers for the seriously handicapped people.

Some voluntary organizations like the Lions Club, Rotary Club, Leo Club, Jaycee Club etc, are rendering good service to the handicapped by giving social grants and assistance like three wheel chairs, crutches, artificial limbs, scholarships for education, finance for sewing machines, free medical tests and treatment to those handicapped (Chintamanikar 1992, Panda 1997, Cruichshank 1968).

SCOPE OF THE STUDY

The present investigation is confined to school for physically handicapped located in Karnataka State only. Out of them school from Dharwad, Bellary, and Chitradurga District were involved in the study. It may be pointed out here that these schools were selected for two reasons. One, all these schools were recognized by the government of Karnataka and are well established and secondly they provide full co-operation to the researchers.

The study is further confined to the children studying in IX standard in schools for physically handicapped.

This study covers the IX standard children achievement in the three core subjects prescribed by the Government of Karnataka like General science, general mathematics and social studies.

LIMITATIONS OF THE STUDY

The researcher is quite aware of the limitations under which the present study was conducted. Hence suggests that no sweeping generalizations could be made, as they have to be viewed in the light of the following limitations:

1. The present study was confined to IX standard children in schools for physically handicapped located in the districts Chitradurga, Bellary and Dharwad.
2. A number of variables influence the academic achievement of physically handicapped children. The present study was confined to only 5 factors. However, certain factors like intelligence, socio-economic status, social maturity, scholastic aptitude, educational aspirations, attitude towards schools environmental factors etc. which might effect the academic achievement were beyond the scope of the present study.
3. The present study is limited only to the IX standard of whose medium of instruction was Kannada.
4. In the present study, the term crippled implies to a boy or girl in the age group of 12 and 18 yrs. who seems to be deviant from the normal in his physical structure.

SUGGESTIONS FOR FURTHER RESEARCH

The researcher by virtue of her experience while studying the present problem offers the following for further research.

1. A study of the factors in relation to academic achievement when, physically handicapped children are classified according to their age, intelligence and socio-economic status etc.
2. A similar study may be taken up with sample drawn from the whole state.
3. A similar study may be taken up at the primary level, pre-university level.
4. A study may be undertaken for the students whose medium of instruction is other than Kannada.

Bibliograpy

Abdul, Test Anxiety, *Journal of Personality and Clinical Studies,* March, vol. 7(1) 1991, pp. 123-124.

Agarwal, J.C., *Essentials of Educational Psychology,* Vikas Publishing House Pvt. Ltd., New Delhi 1994.

Agarwal and Rita, "Study of Anxiety and adjustment levels among the visually and hearing impaired and their relationship to locus of control", *Journal of Psychology,* May, Vol. 119, (3) 1985, pp. 265-269.

Allen Elizabeth, Behavioral Treatment of Anxiety and related disorders in Adults with mental handicap, *Journal of Mental Handicap Research,* January, Vol. 2 (1) 1998.

Anderson and Framer, J., "Self-concept and coping in adolescent with a physical disability," *Journal of Issues in Mental Health-Nursing,* June, Vol. 4(4) 1982, pp. 217-218.

Andreanska, "Specificities of motivation in handicapped children," *Journal of Studies in Psychology,* April, Vol. 23 940 1991, pp 289-276.

Anastasia Anne, *Psychological Testing,* 5th edition, New York. Macmillan Publishing Company, Inc., 1963.

ArtharI.Gates et al., *Educational Psychology,* 3rd edition, Macmillan Company New York, 1942.

Atkinson J.W. and Litwin G.H., Achievement motivation and test Anxiety conceived as motive to approach success and avoid failure, *Journal of Abnormal and Social Psychology*, 1960, pp. 52-53.

Barbara. J., "Study of academic Achievement and Non-verbal intelligence in Public school hearing impaired children." *Journal of Psychology in the Schools*, July, Vol. 27 (3) 1990, pp. 210-217.

Bala, A Comprehensive study of the mental make-up and educational facilities for the physically handicapped and normal children. *Fourth Survey of Research in Education (1983-88)*. Vol. II Published by N.C.E.R.T. 1984.

Basavaraj and Rudrappa, Self-concept, Anxiety, and Adjustment in relation to verbal reasoning, numerical ability reasoning among boys and girls of the 9th standard students, *Indian Psychological Abstract*, Vol. 20, pp. 426.

Bhatnagar, R.P., *A Study of Some of the Personality Variables as Predictors of Academic Achievement*, Doctoral Thesis, Delhi University, 1997.

Bhatia and Bhatia, *A Textbook of Educational Psychology*, Doaba House, New Delhi, pp. 364-367. 1996.

Bharati, The self-concept and Achievement motivation of early Adolescents. *Fourth Survey of Research in Education (1983-1988)*, Vol. I, N.C.E.R.T., 1991.

Berney R.C. and Teevar, R.C., *Measuring Human Motivation* New Jersey. Van Nostrand Inc., 1962.

Binod Kumar Sahu, *Education of the Exceptional Children*, Kalyani Publishers, New Delhi. 1990.

Bloomquist John, "Some social factors and school failures," *International Review of Education* 3, 1957, pp. 105-3.

Bodner et al., "The Study of Family Environment and

Achievement of deaf students." *Journal of Exceptional Children.* Feb, Vol. 52(5) 1986, pp. 443-449.

Brook over W.B. and Thomas, 'Self-concept of ability and school achievement'. *Sociology of Education.* Michigan 1964, pp. 271-278.

Bruce A.C., Indian education in the city correlates of Academic Performance. *Journal of Educational Psychology,* Vol. 70(3), 1977, pp.135-146.

Butch, M.B., A survey of Research in Education, Baroda, Center of advanced study in education, 1974, N.C.E.R.T.

Butch, M.B. (ed.), *Fourth Survey of Research in Education (1983-88),* vol. I and II N.C.E.R.T., New Delhi, 1991.

Campbell P.B., School and self-concept educational leadership *Journal of the Association for the Supervision and Curriculum Development,* Jan, vol. 24, 1967, pp. 501-515.

Captain, H.D., "The relationship between self-concept and Academic Achievement" *Dissertation International Abstract,* 24, 1960, pp. 979-980.

Caplehorn. W. F. and Sultan, A.J., "Need Achievement and its relation to school performance, Anxiety and intelligence," Australia Journal of Psychology, 27, 1980.

Chaube, S.P., *Development Psychology,* Laxmi Narain Agarwal, Agra, 1987.

Chaube, P.and Akilesh Chaube, *Educational Psychology and Experiments,* Himalayan Publishing House, Delhi, 1996.

Chauhan, S.S. *Advanced Educational Psychology,* 6th edition, Vikas Publishing House Pvt. Ltd., 1978, pp. 449-519.

Chaterji, Comparative study of personality, intelligence and achievement motivation of students in different academic groups. *Fourth Survey of Research in Education,* Vol. (1), 1983-88 Baroda, N.C.E.R.T., 1984.

Chawla T.R., Adjustment and Academic Achievement, *Psychological Studies* 15 (1) 1970, pp. 13-16.

Chintamanikar, *Exceptional Children, Their Psychological education,* Sterling Publishers, Pvt. Ltd, New Delhi.

Coleman J.M., Achievement level, social class, and self-concept of mildly handicapped children, *Journal of Learning Disabilities.* Jan, vol. 18(1) 1085, pp. 26-30.

Health impaired and physically disabled children educational implications. *International Journal of Child and Adolescents Psychiatry.* Vol. 55 (10), 1992, pp. 41-44

Davidson. K.S., Interview of parents of high anxious and Low anxious, *Child Development,* 30, 1959.

David G., Myers, Social Psychology, International edition, 1996, pp. 38-39.

Dececco John P. and Crowford William, The Psychology pf learning and Instruction. Educational Psychology, 2nd edition, Prentice-Hall of India Pvt. Ltd., New Delhi, 1977.

Deo Prathibha and Sharma Sagar, Effect of self-concept on Academic Achievement. *Indian Psychological Abstract,* Vol. (4) 1970, pp. 130-137.

Donald Ary, et.al, *Introduction to Research in Education.* Holt Rinehart and Winston inc., New York Chicago, 1972.

Dyson, Lily, L., Adjustment of Siblings of handicapped children. *Journal of Pediatric Psychology.* June, Vol. 14 (2), 1989, pp. 215-225.

Earnest, R. Hilgard, et al., *Introduction of Psychology,* sixth edition, IBM Publishing Co. Pvt. Ltd., Oxford, 1975.

Ebel, R.L. and Noll Y.H., *Encyclopedic of Educational Research,* Macmillan Company, Toronto, 1969.

Ebel, R.L., *Measuring Educational Achievement*, Prentice hall, Inc., Englewood Cliffs, New Jersey, 1965.

Elizabeth, B. Hurlock, *Child Development with International Edition*, McGraw Hill Book Company, 1978, pp. 208.

Elizabeth M.N., Special Educational Service on the self-concept, *Journal Roeper Review*, Sep., Vol. 12(1) 1989, pp. 29-36.

Entwistle, N.J. and Entwistle. D., Study of the relation between personality, study method and academic performance. *British Journal of Educational Psychology*, 49(2),1970, pp. 132-141.

Everett. A. The self-concept of high medium and low academic achievers, *Australia, Journal of Education*. 15, 1972, p. 319-332.

Ferguson, A.G., *Statistical analysis in Psychology and Education*, Fifth edition, McGraw Hill Co., Kogakusha, Ltd., Japan, 1981.

Freeman, S. F., *Theory and Practice of Psychological Testing*. Third edition, Oxford, IBM Publishing Co, pvt. Ltd., New Delhi, 1962.

Gandhi, *Academic Achievement in relation to Achievement motive, affiliation motive and power motive*. Second Survey of Research in Education, N.C.E.R.T., New Delhi, 1979, pp. 663.

Garrett, H.F. Woodworth, R.S., *Statistics in Psychology and Education*. Vakils Feffer and Simons, Pvt. Ltd., Bombay, 1973.

Gardner Lindzly, *Theories of Personality*, Third edition, Wiley Eastern Ltd., New Delhi, 1978.

Garrett H.E., *Statistic in Psychology and Education*, Feyeard Simsons, Pvt. Ltd, Bombay, 1965.

Gates. A. I., *Educational Psychology,* Macmillan Company, New York.

Gay, L.R., *Educational Research,* New York, Maxwell, Macmillan Publishing Company, 1990, pp. 36-37.

Gilbert Sax, Foundation of educational research, Prentice-Hall Inc., Englewood Cliffs. New Jersey, 1979, pp.16-37.

Gillian, A.K., Self Evaluation and self-concept of adolescent with Physical disabilities. *American Journal of Occupational Therapy*. Feb., Vol.(1792). 1993, pp. 132-140.

Goodman, Libby. Efficacy of the visual motor training for orthopaedically handicapped. *Journal, Rehabilitation Literature,* Oct. Vol. 30 (10), 1973, pp. 299-304.

Go swami, P. K., Self-concept of the Adolescence and their relationship with scholastic achievement and adjustment. *Third Survey of Research in Education, (1978-83),* N.C.E.R.T., New Delhi., 1979, pp. 635.

Gough, H. C., Factors relating o the Academic Achievements in the High school Students. *Journal of Educational Psychology* 40, 1949, pp. 65-78.

Gregory, James., Orthopaedically handicapped students in public and private High School. *Journal of Exceptional Child*. July, vol. 34 (2), 1987, pp. 85-92.

Guilford, J.P. and Benjamin Fruchta, *Fundamental Statistics in Psychology and Education,* sixth edition, McGraw Hill Book co., Singapore, 1978, pp. 78, 193. 223-242.

Gyanani, The frustration reactions function of achievement motivation and anxiety at different age levels, *Fourth Survey of Research in Education,* vol. (83-84) Baroda, N.C.E.R.T., 1984.

Hans Raj Bhatia, *Textbook of Educational Psychology*, Waswani S.G. Macmillan Company of India. Ltd., 1977.

Harvey. The self-concept of physically handicapped children and their non-handicapped siblings. *Journal of Child Psychology and Psychiatry and Allied Discipline*, Apr, Vol. 25(2). 1984, pp. 273-284.

Harvey Davis and Greenway Philip. How parent's attitude and Emotional reactions affect their handicapped children self-concept. *Journal of Psychological Medicine*, May, Vol. 12(2) 1982, pp. 357-370.

Hasnian, Attempted to study the effect pf self-concept on levels of academic achievement and school backgrounds. *Journal of Psychological Research* Sept., Vol. 26(3) 1982, pp. 146-149.

Hassenuddin., *A Comparative Approach of Normal and Handicapped Children*, Ashish Publishing House, New Delhi, 1995.

Hasnian, et al., Study of self-disclosure, anxiety and ascendance submission among physically handicapped and normal students. *Journal of Psychological Research* Sept, Vol. 26(3) 1982, pp. 146-149.

Hal Allen and Kaufman., *Exceptional Children*, Prentice-Hall, Englewood Cliffs, New Jersey, 1978, pp. 379-428.

Henry–claylindgren., *Educational Psychology in the classroom.* Printed in U.S.A., 1976.

Herbert Sorenson. *Psychology in Education*, University of Kentucky, McGraw Hill, Book Company, Toronto, New York, 1954.

Hirunval, A. *A study of pupils self-concept, Academic motivation., classroom climate and academic–performance*, Doctoral Thesis, Mysore University, 1980.

Hopper Chris., Self–concept and Motor performance of hearing impaired boys and girls. *Journal Adapted Physical Activity Quarterly*, Oct., Vol. 5(4), 1988, pp. 292-304.

Hessian. M.G., *Problems and Potentials of the Handicapped*, Atlantic Publishers and Distributors, New Delhi. 1985.

Indrani, Relationship between Academic achievement and achievement motivation of the 9th std. Students. *Abstract of Education Research* (1974-940 Dept. of Extension Service. (R.V. Teachers College.) Bangalore, 1985.

Jain and Pandit, Self-concept and identification of academic goals. *Indian Journal of Applied Psychology*. Aug., Vol. 27(2), 1990, pp. 72-74.

James, M.H. Academic Achievement, Problem reliability of measures for students with mild mental retardation, *Journal of Special Services in the Schools*, Vol. 5(12 0. 1988, pp. 23-31.

James M. Kaufman and Daniel., Handbook of special education, Prentice-Hall Inc. Eaglewood Cliffs, New Jersey, 1978, pp. 248.

John W. Best. *Research in Education*, sixth edition, Prentice-Hall of India, Pvt. Ltd., New Delhi, pp. 8-10 and 110-123.

Jones Reginald. Correlates of orthopaedically disabled children school Achievement and interpersonal relationships, *Journal of Exceptional Children*, Nov 1974. Vol. 41 (3) pp. 191-192.

Kasha, A.C, and Pures, G.S., *Educational Psychology—Guidance and Counseling*, Malhotra, S.N. Donaber House, Nai, serak, Delhi, 1969.

Jaitly, Self-concept of the Physically Handicapped, *Journal of Vocational and Educational Guidance*, Vol. 15 (2), 1972.

James, M.H., Academic Achievement, Problem Reliability of Measures for Students with Mild Mental Retardation, *Journal of Special Services in the Schools*, Vol. 51 2, 1988, pp. 23-31.

James M. Kaufman and Daniel., *Handbook of Special Education*, Prentice-Hall, Inc., Englewood Cliffs, New Jersey, 1978, pp. 24.

John. W. Best, *Research In Education*, sixth Edition, Prentice-Hall of India, Pvt. Ltd., New Delhi, pp. 8-10 and 110-123.

Jones Reginald, Correlates of orthopaedically disabled children school Achievement and interpersonal relationships, *Journal of Exceptional Children*, Nov. 1974. Vol. 41(3), pp. 191-192.

Kashyapa, A.C. And puree, G.S., *Educational Psychology-Guidance and Counseling*, S.N. Donaber House, NAI, Serak, Delhi, 1969.

Knox Wilma. Program on state trait Anxiety and self-ideal concept. *Journal of Psychological Reports*, June, Vol. 34, 1974, pp. 689-690.

Kochhar, S.K., *Educational and Vocational Guidance in Secondary School*, Sterling Publishers Pvt. Ltd., New Delhi, 1993.

Kundu and Tutu. *Educational Psychology*, Sterling Publishers Pvt. Ltd., New Delhi, 1988.

Ladislaw Doric., *Essentials of Educational Psychology*, Sterling Publishers Pvt. Ltd., New Delhi 1988.

Lata, Impact of parental Attitude on Handicapped and normal students in different areas of adjustment. *Fourth Survey of Education in Research*, N.C.E.R.T., 1991.

Lawrence, Self-concept formation and physical handicap, some educational implication for integration, *Journal of*

Disability Handicap in Society, Vol. 6(2). and 1991, pp. 139-146.

Lebo M.D., Scheduling—An approach for students with difficulties in studying. *Journal of the American College Health Associating*, Vol. 22(3). 1974, pp. 242-247.

Lindquist, E.F, *Statistical Analysis in Educational Research*, Oxford, and IBM Publishing Co., New Delhi, 1940.

Lyndall, N. R., Educationally handicapped children, Locus of control and reaching achievement, *Journal of Exceptional Children*, Nov. Vol. and 48(3). 1981, pp. 244-248.

Mahesh Bhargava, *Introduction to Exceptional Children*, Sterling Publishers Pvt. Ltd., New Delhi, 1994.

Mamatha, The correlative study of achievement motivation in relation to self-concept, adjustment problems, in 9th std. Students. *Fourth Survey of Research in Education*.Vol.(1) 83-88, Baroda, N.C.E.R.T., 1992.

Mangal, S.K. *General Psychology*, Sterling Publishers Pvt. Ltd., New Delhi, 1996.

Mathur, S.S. *Educational Psychology*, Vinod Pustak Mandir Publications, Agra, 1979.

Matson Gaylon, Anxiety in visually handicapped children and youth, *Journal of Clinical Child Psychology*, vol. 15(4), 1986, pp.356-359.

Mathur Abha. Comparative study of the adjustment problem, Aspirations, Self-concept and Academic Achievement of handicapped and normal children D.Phil. Education. All university. *Fourth Survey of Research in Education* Vol. (II), N.C.E.R.T., 1985, pp. 1330-31.

Mavrin Cavor, A comparison of the Attitude of mothers of non-handicapped children. *International Journal of Rehabilitation Research*, Vol. 9(4), 1986, pp. 315-324.

Mehrotra, The relationship between intelligence, Socio-economic status, Anxiety, Personality Adjustment and Academic Achievement of high school, Doctoral Thesis, Karnataka University, 1986.

Mehata, D.S. *Handbook of Disabled in India,* Allied Publishers Pvt. Ltd., New Delhi, 1993.

Mehata P.H., The self-concept in Bright under achieving male high school students. *Journal Indian Educational Review,* 3 1968, pp. 100.

Michael., The Self-concept of the mild handicapped and the role of social comparison. *Journal of Special Education,* Aug 1983, Vol. 18(2), pp. 30-42.

Michael, effect of achievement level, social class and the self-concept of mildly handicapped, children. *Journal of Special Education.* Sept: Vol. 17 (1) 1985, pp. 37-45.

Mohanty, The effects of state trait Anxiety on classroom learning and personal adjustment of elementary school pupils. *Second Survey of Research in Education,* N.C.E.R.T., 1985.

Morgan, C. *Introduction to Psychology,* Seventh edition. Tata McGraw-Hill Publishing Company Ltd., New Delhi,1993.

Murphy Harry, Academic Achievementof impaired students, Journal of American Annals-Jan, Vol. 21 (3), 1996, pp. 4.

Muthayya B.C. "Some correlates of Achievement motivation among High and low achieving in the Scholastic field," *Journal of Psychological Research,* Vol. 9 (2), 1965, pp. 89-92.

Norman E. Greenland. *Measurement and Evaluation in Teaching,* eighth edition, Macmillan Publishing Co., New York, 1990, pp.

Norman. L. Munn., *Introduction to Psychology,* Third edition, Oxford and IBH Publishing Co., Pvt. Ltd., New Delhi, 1990.

Olivia., Enhancement of Self-concept and achievement Motivation at the first year degree students. *Fourth Survey of Research in Education,* Vol. (1) 1983-88 Baroda, N.C.E.R.T., 1984, pp. 407-487.

Padhi., Relationship among classroom environment, creativity, academic self-concept and academic achievement. *Indian Journal of Applied Psychology,* July, Vol. 28(2), 1991, pp. 97-100.

Padmapriya.V. A comparative study of Deaf and Normal children, cognitive factors and Academic Achievement. *Journal of Indian Psychology,* Jan., Vol. 7 (1) 1988

Parameshwaran, C, B, *Invitation to Psychology.* Tata McGraw Hill Publishing Co., New Delhi. 1988.

Pandey. The affectional deprivation ego strength and adjustment pattern among visually handicapped children and their relationship. *Fourth Survey of Research in Education,* N.C.E.R.T., 1998.

Parsricha. P. *Educational Psychology,* First Edition, M.S. University, Baroda, 1963.

Pliner, et.al, the role of achievement in teacher's attitude toward handicapped children. *Journal of Academic Psychology Bulletin,* Vol. 7 (3). 1985, Delhi, 1935.

Porter Mach Lon, E., "Exceptional children", *Journal of Exceptional Children,* Mar. 1980, Vol. 46 (6), pp. 77-78.

Presley let al, *Psychology in Education,* Sidney Universal Bookstall, Delhi 1981.

Rai. B.C., *Educational Psychology,* Prakashan Kendra, Railway crossing Sitapur road, Lucknow Reynolds.M.and

Davids.M., Exceptional children in regular class room, M.S,university, Minnesota Press, 1971.

Roessler Richard., An Evaluation of personal and skill training with visually handicapped, *Journal of Rehabilitation in Counseling Bulletin*, June, Vol. 21(4), 1978, pp. 305-380.

Roser Howell., Physically disabled and Achievement orientation self-concept, *Journal of Vocational Behavior*, Aug. Vol. 13(1), 1978, pp. 35-44.

Roswell., "Positive reinforcement program on the self-concept," *Journal American Correction Therapy*, July-Aug., Vol. 40 (4) 1986, pp. 91-94.

Saraswat, Self-concept in relation to the adjustment, values of academic achievement. Socio-economic. Status and sex of high school students of Delhi. *Indian Educational Review*, Vol. 20(3), July 1985.

Saraswat, Self-concept in relation to the adjustment, values of academic achievement. Socio-economic status and sex of high school students of Delhi. *Indian Educational Review*, Vol. 20 (3), July 1985.

Saraswati R.K, *Self Concept*, Scale National Psychological Corporation, Agra 1984.

Schertz :Investigated the self concept of expressive language of adolescent hearing impaired student using the Q-sort technique. *Journal, American Annals of the Deaf*, Dec. Vol. 120(8) 1975, pp. 572-577

Schertz, Jane, "Self-concept of handicapped," *Journal, American Annals of Deaf.*, Dec 1975. Vol. 120(6).

Shanti Nayal, et.al., Self-concept and class adjustment of adolescent in relation to their sex, school discipline, income group and academic achievement. *Indian Education Review*, Vol. 24(2), April 1989.

Shanmugan. T. E., *Abnormal Psychology,* first reprint, Tata McGraw Hill Publ., Co. Ltd., New Delhi, 1985, pp. 158.

Sharma and Bhatt.B.D., *Education of the Gifted and Talented Children.* Kanishka Publishing House, Delhi, 1993, pp. 1, 127, 235.

Singh, S.D. The pattern, achievement and adjustment of mentally superior children. *Fourth Survey of Research in Education,* Vol. II., 1985, N.C.E.R.T.

Sinha, D. *Sinha Anxiety scale,* Varshini Rupa Psycological Corporation 1996.

Skinner, E. *Educational Psycology.* Prentice Hall of India, Pvt. Ltd.

Smith, et.al., Effects of co-operative individualistic instruction on the achievement of handicapped. *Journal of Social Psychology,* April, 1982, Vol. 116 (2). Minneapolis, pp. 277-283.

Srinivasam T. A study of divergent thinking and scholastic achievement of deaf and dumb students. *Journal of Child Psychiatry,* July, Sept., 1980. Vol. 21(30).

Suoer John. T. Self-concept and need for achievement of men with physical disabilities, *Journal of General Psychology,* Jan., Vol. 119 (1), pp. 73-80.

Timberlake, Elizabeth. M. a). self-concept protection by children with physical differences. *Journal of Child and Adolescent Social Work,* Vol. 2(4). 1985, pp. 232-246. (b) Motivational and Effective differences among normally achieveing, learning disabled developmentally handicapped. *Journal of Clinical Psychology,* Sept. Vol. 21(3) 1993, pp. 229-239.

Truzuki, Self-concept in Non-handicapped and intellectually

handicapped Japanese, *Journal of Special Education* Oct., Vol.19(2)1981, pp. 29-37.

Tuckman Bruce W. *Conducting Educational Research,* New York Harcourt braco Javanvich Inc., 1978.

Uday Shankar. *Exceptional Children,* Sterling Publishers Pvt. Ltd., New Delhi, 1984.

Webber Gall, Y. Visual disabilities, their identification and relationship with academic achievement. *Journal of Learning Disabilities,* July, Vol. 13 (6), 1980.

Weller, et al, Assessing the effects of experimental studies on the self concept of the preadolescent physically handicapped. *Journal of American Corrective Therapy,* Nov. Dec., Vol. 39 96), 1985 state, pp. 134-140.

Reynold James. G. "Fear and Anxiety, Low Vision of totally blind children," *Journal of Education of the Visually Handicapped,* Vol. 20(4),1989.

Wrong Bernicey, Motivation for learning in mildly handicapped adolescents, *Journal Exceptional Education,* Quarterly, Aug. Vol. 1 (2) 1980, pp. 37-45.

TABLE X(APPEN)

NUMBERS OF STATEMENTS SELECTED FOR ADJUSTMENT INVENTORY WITH THEIR CHI-S OTHERS TITLES

1. Study related to the development of Self-concept Achievement, Motivation, Adjustment and Unanxiety among the phygicaly handicapped children studying in Secondary Schools of Karnataka.

2. Study related to the factors affecting on a Achievement, of physically handicapped children studying in Secondary Schools of Karnataka.

Index

A

AAMD (American Association of Mental Deficiency), 3
Academic Achievement, 20, 30, 31, 32, 34, 35, 37-40, 43, 45-50, 52-57, 63-65, 95-102, 104-112, 115, 116, 118-120, 124
Achievement Motivation, 23, 31, 34, 37, 38, 47, 48, 49, 54-57, 61, 62, 98-100, 102, 106-109, 113, 119
Achievement Motivation Groups, 113
Adjustment, 59
  All Types, 51
  Areas Included, 83
  Educational, 51, 63
  Emotional, 63
  Health, 51, 63
  Home, 51, 63
  Inventory, 83-87, 89
  Problem, 1, 50, 55, 82
  School, 51
  Social, 51, 63
American Males with Physical Disabilities, 43
Anxiety
  Groups, 96, 97, 101, 106-108, 111, 119
  Motivation, 106, 109
  Reactions to, 61
  Scale, 44
Artificial Limbs, 14
Autonomous Achievements, 47

B

Bangalore City, 49
Bellary Dist., 55, 88, 90, 133
Bells Adjustment, 49
Britain and USA, 64

C

California State University, 45
Characteristics,
  Mental, 2
  Physical, 2, 4
  Psychological, 4
Childhood Activities, 10
  Educational, 10
  Social Recreational, 10
  Vocational, 10
Children, 1
  Classification, 6
    Blind, 6
    Deaf, 6
    Dumb, 6
  Deviated, 1

Exceptional, 1-5
  Classification, 2
    Gifted, 2
    Mentally Handicap, 2
    Physically Handicap, 2
  Definition, 2
Chitradurga Dist, 55, 88, 90, 133
Chi-Square Value, 85, 86
Civilization, 68
CMR (Custodial/Dependent Mentally)4
Cognitive
  Ability, 4
  Factors, 46
Control Group, 42
Correlation Techniques, 50
Crippled Children, 13, 14, 15, 18, 19, 28-31, 50-52, 67, 68, 90
  Adjustment Problems, 18, 30, 35, 37
  Characteristics, 15, 37
  Classification, 14
  Identification, 16, 17, 37
  Problems, 13
Crippled Nature Causes, 15
  Acquired, 15
  Congenital, 15
  Hereditary, 15
Crippled Students, 66, 68
Cultural Organization, 62

D

Defeatism, 25
Delhi Administration, 40
Deo-Mohan's Achievement Motivation Scale, 69
Dharwad Dist., 55, 88, 90, 133
Disability, 7, 11, 12
Disability Population Table, 13
Disabled Children, 12, 18
Disadvantaged Groups, 12
Dix, Doratheo, 7

E

Education Commission, (1964-66), 5
Education, 1, 4, 6, 11, 12, 26-31, 125, 128, 132
  Elementary, 12
  Exceptional Children, 5, 26
  Expansion of-, 7
  Informal, 27
  Modern, 125
  Of Crippled Children, 28, 29
  Of Deaf, 7
  Universalization free and Compulsory, 125
  Universalization of Elementary-, 12
Educational
  Achievement Test, 71,72, 81
  and Physical Needs, 28
  and Vocational Training, 29
  Problems, 7, 51
  Services, 4
Elementary School Children, 41
Emotional and Social Adjustment, 27, 28
EMR (Educational Mentally Retarded), 3
England and America, 12
Europe, 7
Exceptional Children (Child), 5, 6, 26, 27, 35, 117
Experimental Group, 42

G

Gestalt, 58, 59
Gifted Children, 4

H

Handicap Children, 10, 11, 12, 31, 34, 35, 39, 46, 47, 50, 55, 130, 132
  In India, 11
  In Karnataka, 11, 12

Handicap Definition, 9

Handicap Schools, 66, 68, 69

Health and Welfare, M/O, 133

High Achievement Motivation Groups, 113

High Adjustment Groups, 103, 105, 107, 111-113, 115, 119

High Anxiety, 97, 98, 107, 108, 111

Holders, William, 7

Homicide and Suicide, 26

Hotel Kere, 83

Howe, 7

Human Resource Development, M/O, 11

Hypothesis of the Survey, 56-58

I

Index of Indiscrimination, 76, 77

K

Karnataka State, 55, 65, 72, 90, 133, 134

Kuppuswamy's Scale, 49

L

Low Achievement Motivation Groups, 108, 114

Low Anxiety, 97, 98, 107

M

Malebennur, 83

Mann, Horace, 7

Medical Aids, 29

Medieval Church, 7

Mehta Achievement Motivation Test, 48

Mental Retardation, 3

Mentally Handicap Children, 3

Mentally Handicap, 11

Mentally Retarded, 12, 13

Middle Ages, 7

N

Nagpur, 43

National Policy on Education, 5, 132, 133

NSS (National Sample Survey), 11

O

Orthopaedically Handicap (Children), 14, 35, 37, 45

P

Personality Problem, 26

Physical Disability, 43

Physically (Crippled) Children, 117

Physically Disability, 22

Physically Handicap, 90, 98, 133
  Adjustment Problems, 55
  Children, 3, 6, 7, 9, 10, 13, 17, 18, 32, 34, 35, 38, 39, 41, 42, 44, 51-57, 82, 96-101, 104, 106-109, 111, 112, 117-120
  Classification, 10
  Concept of-, 7
  Historical Backgrous, 6
  Students, 106, 109, 116

Pithoragarh and Nainital (UP), 43

Planning Programme, 15

Prayag Mehta Achievement Motivation Inventory, 49
Projective Measures, 71
Prosthetic Devices, 14
Psychological Disorders, 11
Psycho-Social Development, 18
Public Schools, 43
Punjab University, 39

R

Rao Socio-Economic Status Scale, 48, 49
Raven's Standard Progressive Matrices, 46
Recreational Needs, 132
Retarded Children, 46
Rogers' Theory, 58, 59
Rousseau, 7

S

Sampling Techniques, 54
School Organizational Atmosphere, 28
School,
  Adjustment, 2
  Children, 1
  Organizational Atmosphere, 28
  Placement, 4
  Residential, 27
  System, 12
  Traditional—Program, 5
Scientific and Technical Development, 31
SDS Kurtosis and Shewner, 39
Self-Concept, 19-21, 41-43, 48, 51, 54, 55, 57, 58, 59, 66, 67, 94-96, 98, 101-105, 118, 124-126
  Definition, 58
  Square, 96, 97, 99, 104
  Scale, 42, 49
Sensory Abilities, 2
SES, 40, 48, 49
Siddalingeswara Residential Integrated Handicap Schools, 73
Skills,
  Academic, 3
  Cognitive, 64
  Communication, 4
  Vocational, 3
Social Agencies, 62
Social and Emotional, 1
  Behaviour, 2
  Needs, 1
Social Comparison
  Group, 42
  Theory, 41
Social Status, 64
Society, 3, 5, 6, 29, 30, 31, 132
  West, 64
Socio-Cultural Environment, 5
Socio-Economic Status, 40
Sparta, 6
Special Education, 5-7, 10
Sports Activities, 28
State Legislation, 14
Statistical Techniques, 54, 90

T

Teaching Aids, 130
Teaching Methods and Programmes, 26
Tennessee Self Concept Scale, 43
Thematic Apperception Test, 43
TMR (Trainable or Mentally Retarded), 3
Training Vocational Guidance, 27

U

United Nations, 9

Universities, 31

V

Vocational Rehabilitation Centres, 133

Vocational Training, 132

Voluntary Organizations, 133

W

Wallis, John, 7

World Health Organization, 3, 8

❑❑❑